Silent Rosary

Silent Rosary

A Contemplative, Exegetical, and Iconographic Tour Through the Mysteries

Addison Hodges Hart

Original icons by
Solrunn Nes

CASCADE *Books* • Eugene, Oregon

SILENT ROSARY
A Contemplative, Exegetical, and Iconographic Tour Through the Mysteries

Cascade Books
An Imprint of Wipf and Stock Publishers
199 W. 8th Ave., Suite 3
Eugene, OR 97401

www.wipfandstock.com

PAPERBACK ISBN: 978-1-7252-7232-3
HARDCOVER ISBN: 978-1-7252-7231-6
EBOOK ISBN: 978-1-7252-7233-0

Cataloguing-in-Publication data:

Names: Hart, Addison Hodges, author. | Nes, Solrunn, illustration.

Title: Silent Rosary : a contemplative, exegetical, and iconographic tour through the mysteries / by Addison Hodges Hart ; illustrations by Solrunn Nes.

Description: Eugene, OR: Cascade Books, 2021

Identifiers: ISBN 978-1-7252-7232-3 (paperback) | ISBN 978-1-7252-7231-6 (hardcover) | ISBN 978-1-7252-7233-0 (ebook)

Subjects: LCSH: Rosary. | Mysteries of the Rosary.

Classification: BX2163 .H32 2021 (print) | BX2163 (ebook)

06/24/21

(Unless otherwise noted, biblical quotations throughout this book are taken from the Revised Standard Version.)

(Photography: Lars Arvid Oma)

But we all, with open face beholding as in a glass [a metallic mirror] *the glory of the Lord, are changed into the same image from glory to glory, even as by the Spirit of the Lord . . . For God, who commanded the light to shine out of darkness, hath shined in our hearts, to give the light of the knowledge of the glory of God in the face of Jesus Christ.*

—2 Corinthians 3:18; 4:6 (KJV)

The kingdom of God is not coming as something to be observed, nor will persons say, "Behold: here it is" or "There it is," for behold, the kingdom of God is within you.

—Luke 17:20b–21 (my translation)

A man that looks on glass,
On it may stay his eye;
Or if he pleaseth, through it pass,
And then the heav'n espy.

—George Herbert, "The Elixir"

Contents

Part One: Entering the Circular Gallery

Part Two: The Twenty Mysteries

Part One

Entering the Circular Gallery

"Mysteries"

I begin with a caveat. This is not a book about the rosary as such. That is to say, it is not about the mechanics of the devotion, nor is it a guide or manual or even an appeal to use it in one's practice of prayer. Rather, this is a book about what are usually termed the *mysteries* of the rosary, those twenty (originally fifteen—see below) stories or narratives or pictures that are derived—all except the final two—from the Gospels in the New Testament.

What initially kindled our imagination for producing this book was a simple idea: my wife, iconographer Solrunn Nes, and I wished to collaborate on a project together. She would provide the art and I would write the accompanying text. What we were looking for was a single coherent, interconnected arrangement of images that would hang together naturally—a sequence that possessed diversity and yet was a unified whole. At some point in our search, we struck upon the sequence of the mysteries of the rosary, and although we considered other possible projects, this seemed ideal for the sort we conceived.

Solrunn's artwork throughout this volume is in the Byzantine iconographic style that is her specialty.[1] Iconography by intention is not a realistic form of art. It is rich in symbol and visual metaphor. To understand it for what it is, on its own terms, requires appreciation of its symbols and stylistic peculiarities, and it only opens up its secrets through the exercising of more than one sense of interpretation by the viewer (more on that in due course). It is a "spiritual" art, if one will forgive the somewhat clichéd

1. For more about her art—how it is made, the elements of its style, its symbolism, and more—see Nes, *The Mystical Language of Icons*.

sound of that; but what that means in this case is that its true aim is not aesthetic, though, of course, aesthetics is important. Its essential purpose is to involve the viewer—who approaches it in the right frame of mind—at a profound level, one that certainly goes deeper than "art appreciation." An icon is, in common with all forms of sacred art worldwide, something to be *read* and *interpreted*. In that sense, it is indeed like a text, best read in receptive silence. And if it has been rightly engaged, it at length disappears to the viewer much as a windowpane "disappears" as one's concentration passes through it to the scene on the other side of the glass.

In deciding to work with the mysteries of the rosary, we were also aware that the rosary as a devotional item is not something that everyone welcomes unreservedly. Certainly, it comes with "baggage." It is distinctly a Roman Catholic devotion, for one thing, although many Protestants and Anglicans use it regularly. It puts an emphasis on Mary, Mother of the Lord—which, for some, is an objectionable focus. The rosary also has a checkered record of historical associations that some find off-putting. It has, for instance, a celebrated connection with war. The Catholic Church annually recalls the Battle of Lepanto every October 7, when on that date in 1571 the Holy League defeated the fleet of the Ottoman Empire in the Gulf of Patras. This victory inflicted on the Turks was piously believed to have been directly due to an intense program promoting the praying of the rosary. And it gave the Church yet another Marian feast day: "Our Lady of Victory," subsequently renamed "Our Lady of the Most Holy Rosary." A century before that event, one of the great promoters of the rosary as a devotion, the Dominican Jacobus Springer, a disciple of Alain de la Roche (see below), had also been one of the two authors of the *Malleus Maleficarum* ("Hammer of Witches"), the textbook for witch-hunting not only used by zealous Dominicans in Springer's era, but in a later age by Protestant witch-hunters as well.[2] (With promoters like that, one might say, who needs gainsayers?) And, lastly, one might justifiably see in the Church's official sanctioning of the "heaven-bestowed" rosary one more manifestation of the unfortunate "suppression of silence" which occurred under institutional Church supervision in a deliberate attempt to eradicate such contrived "heresies" as "Quietism" (considered threatening to ecclesial order). With its increasingly wordy additions (for example, the recitation of the Apostles' Creed, Marian antiphons, and other prayers as various customs developed),

2. MacCulloch, *Christianity*, 686. See also Huizinga, *Autumn of the Middle Ages*, 232–33.

its emphasis on "discursive meditation" rather than receptive silence, and its elaborate (and much too conscious) mechanics in a "proper" manipulating of crucifix, appended medal, big beads, smaller beads, and chain, it was the "safe" alternative to spiritual practices not as easily controlled. Interior prayer, personal encounter and revelation, and contemplation in silence have often been viewed as threatening in authoritarian contexts. Beginning in earnest in the fifteenth century, the Western Church's intensifying endeavors to control individuals' prayer lives, to inhibit and arraign (and, on occasion, execute) those exhibiting ardent "mystical" and lively contemplative tendencies, is documented well by Maggie Ross.[3] The rosary as a tool, seen in this light, might well be implicated. It appeared in the form it has retained ever since within the context of what Huizinga described as "the decay of the strongly colored piety of the late medieval period [which was like] the form of a flower past its prime."[4]

And yet, that cannot be the whole story. Generation after generation has found in the rosary consolation, insight, and—in those most valued moments—the undeniable presence of the holy. Who can dispute that? Despite its association with a sixteenth-century naval battle, or a fifteenth-century bloodstained fanatical proponent of the devotion, or its exploitation as an institutionally endorsed devotional instrument, despite *all that* (and more), the simple fact remains that countless sincere believers have used the rosary to excellent effect for a very long time. That makes it worth taking seriously by those of us inclined to be critical, and—further—we may want to consider what there is in it that fires the imaginations of its users. Arguably, at least to my mind, the aspect of the rosary most positively influential in the lives of believers has been its circular "gallery" of images known as "mysteries."

It is with the mysteries, as I have already noted, that this book is concerned, and not with the sensible rosary as such (though I touch on that briefly below). One could, in fact, approach these mysteries without the rosary at all. One can encounter them simply, contemplatively, silently, without beads in hand, and still find in this interlocking series of images, stories, parables, and "mirrors" an undeniable power. Like the shape of the rosary itself, the twenty mysteries are a gallery circular in configuration. One makes the full rounds, so to speak, taking in each image, and then

3. Ross, *Silence (Volume 1)*, 126–220. I am indebted to Maggie Ross for both volumes of her *Silence: A User's Guide* throughout this introductory chapter, as shall be evident.

4. Huizinga, *Autumn of the Middle Ages*, 232.

returns to the beginning and starts all over again. It is, as I suggested above, also a bit like a hall of mirrors. Each mystery on the surface depicts an event taken from the narratives, canonical and non-canonical, about Christ. With time and repetition, though, we discover that each mystery also reflects our selves, in particular those areas within us that we usually do not see or even have become adept at avoiding. In such a sustained contemplative practice of "beholding," conducted in silence, we begin to engage our "heart"—the term the Bible uses for the deepest level of our psyche. We come to find it reflected back to us in these images. There are, of course, many modes of prayer that can put us deeply in touch with Spirit; the mysteries of the rosary can effectively be one of those ways.

The word *mysteries* is a confusing word, sounding rather arcane to modern ears. However, as is also true of its use in the New Testament, the word refers to something hidden or veiled, but now made known or revealed. So, for instance, the Letter to the Ephesians refers to the revelation of Christ as "the mystery hidden for ages in God who created all things," and the Letter to the Colossians speaks of "the mystery hidden for ages and generations but now made manifest" (Eph 3:9; Col 1:26). It is the aspect of its being made "manifest" that defines the nature of a "mystery," in its Christian context, as much as its former "hiddenness." A "mystery" is fittingly understood, then, as a vehicle by which the divine is "unveiled" to the human person, or, better, *within* the human person ("God, who commanded the light to shine out of darkness, hath shined *in our hearts*, to give the light of the knowledge of the glory of God in the face of Jesus Christ"—2 Cor 4:6). It "opens up" the human mind to God and, with that, a concomitant "opening up" of the person to himself or herself ("For now we see in a mirror dimly . . ."—1 Cor 13:12). Perhaps a better word than "mystery," then, might simply be "revelation" or, perhaps better yet, "insight." The latter word indicates an "inward seeing" or—passing beyond the veil of the Temple, so to speak—a "seeing into" what lies beyond. It is a vision that penetrates deeper than the surface of things. We shall come back to this in due course.

A Very Brief History of the Rosary

It is appropriate here, before moving on to other related matters, to take a cursory look at the history of the rosary itself. After all, if there had been no custom of a string of beads used in prayer there would never have been a complementary string of mysteries to contemplate. The latter grew out of the former.

The use of beads (or knots or pebbles) in prayer predates Christianity, of course, and finds parallels in Hinduism, Buddhism, and Islam. Its beginnings in Christian practice are obscure, but the custom existed in ancient times among desert monastics. The Christian East has its prayer rope, often made from wool, with knots or beads or a combination of both. The prayer rope (called a *komvoschinion* in Greek and a *tchotki* in Russian) involves repetition of the "Jesus Prayer" ("Lord Jesus Christ, Son of God, have mercy on me, a sinner") or one of its variants, sometimes interspersed on colored or larger beads with invocations addressed to the Mother of God. Unlike the Western rosary, there are no mental visualizations—no "mysteries"—accompanying these prayers. Rather, in the use of the prayer rope, the mind is supposed to be focused on the *words* of the Jesus Prayer. This concentrated recitation is used to guard one's thoughts from intrusive mental images and other distracting thoughts.

The Western rosary took shape during the Middle Ages with the use of strings of beads by the unlettered laity who did not participate in the choir office with the local monks. The word *bead*, in fact, has its roots in the old Germanic word meaning to "beseech," "entreat," or "pray." In Medieval English this became *beda*, and, in modern English, *bid*. It was the name by which the "Venerable" Bede, the Anglo-Saxon monastic saint and scholar, was called (an unusual name, although a monk of Lindisfarne also possessed it). Instead of the 150 Psalms that the more literate monks chanted in choir, lay brothers attached to the monasteries substituted 150 *Pater Nosters* ("Our Fathers"), and this custom spread to the laity in general. The practice was known as "the poor man's Psalter." By the early thirteenth century there had developed a parallel "Our Lady's Psalter" of 150 *Aves* (the "Hail Mary" in its original form), which replaced the monastic practice of reciting a special daily "office"—over and above the "canonical hours (offices)" outlined in the monastic Rule—to honor Mary (the so-called "Little Office of the Blessed Virgin Mary").

The "Hail Mary" at this stage of its development was the uniting of Gabriel's salutation of Mary with that of Elizabeth's (Luke 1:28, 42). The name of Jesus was added to the "Hail Mary," given the potency ascribed to his name by both Western and Eastern Christians. The number of beads on a string was eventually reduced in most cases from 150 to 50 and regularly prayed three times daily (morning, noon, and evening). Each "decade" of beads was interspersed by a bead called the *paternoster*, which planted firmly the "Our Father" between every set of ten *Aves*.

The florid name *rosarium*—"rose garden"—made its appearance sometime in the middle of the thirteenth century, that age of extravagant and chivalric expression in Western Europe. By the fifteenth century the Dominican Alain de la Roche, also known as Alanus de Rupe (1428–1475), proposed fifteen mysteries as images for mental prayer during the praying of the beads. These were a sequence of scenes taken mostly from the Gospels as a way of ruminating on the incarnation, passion, and glorification of Christ. By the sixteenth century the Doxology to the Holy Trinity (the *Gloria*) was added to the end of each decade, and the traditional fifteen mysteries of the rosary became the set norm for praying the rosary for the next five centuries. Also during the sixteenth century, the familiar concluding portion of the "Hail Mary" was added (*Sancta Maria, Mater Dei, ora pro nobis peccatoribus, nunc et in hora mortis nostrae*; "Holy Mary, Mother of God, pray for us sinners, now and at the hour of our death"). It was a sort of *memento mori*, a remembrance that death awaits us all, and a constant prayer for Mary's protection whenever one's end should come.

In 2002 Pope John Paul II added the five "luminous mysteries"—based on a set of mysteries set down by (Saint) George Preca of Malta (1880–1962)—to the long-established three sets of five (called "Joyful," "Sorrowful," and "Glorious" respectively), bringing the total number of mysteries to twenty. These new mysteries had the effect of filling an obvious gap and bringing more balance to the whole sequence, which, before their addition, simply jumped from the stories of Jesus' birth and childhood directly to his passion and death. Obviously, the devotion had never been intended as an exhaustive arrangement of Gospel scenes, but the "Luminous" mysteries had the effect of putting a formerly neglected focus on (at least a few of) the accounts of Jesus' acts in the Gospels.

So, whether it came about by accident or design (actually, it was a bit of both), the entire series, as it now exists, is notable for its spiritual coherence. As already noted, it has a "circular" configuration. It begins, for example, with the image of the Virgin Mother receiving the eternal Word into her flesh and into the world, and it ends with the image of the Word-made-flesh receiving the Virgin Mother into his glory. It begins with the descent of Christ and ends with the ascent of both Christ and, in Mary, the embodiment of creation renewed. It is, in its shape, the descent/ascent model we find in Philippians 2:5–11 (to which we will return), encompassing the tremendous interwoven themes of incarnation, revelation, *kenosis*, and regeneration (to which we will also return). In short, it is the gospel presented in miniature.

With this background in mind, then, we turn from the history of the rosary as a devotion in the Western church, and give our attention once more, and more closely, to the twenty mysteries. Before that, we must consider the central role the Virgin Mary plays in these mysteries, not only as subject but, even more importantly, as symbol. Appearing as she does at the beginning and end of the "circle," she is what binds the whole loop together. Even when she is not "front and center" in a mystery, she is still "present" (reinforced, of course, when the beads are used, with the repetition of the "Hail, Mary"). We must ask, then, what her presence signifies throughout the sequence.

The Significance of Mary

> "Who shall find a valiant woman? Far from the uttermost coasts is the price of her" (Prov. 31:10) . . . [S]urely we can understand that the valiant woman is the wisdom of God, either Mary, the mother of Wisdom itself, or the Church, mother of the wise, or certainly, the soul as the seat of wisdom. God's wisdom is called a woman because of the fruitfulness of all good things that flow from her. For it is she who announces: "I am the mother of fair love, and of fear, and of knowledge, and of holy hope" (Sirach 24:24).[1]

In these few lines from a sermon of Adam of Perseigne (c. 1145–1221), a Cistercian abbot (and sometime confessor of King Richard the Lionheart), we get a sample of the many connotations that the name and image of Mary had possessed from the church's earliest centuries. Clustered about her was a rich assortment of images—all of them conceptually linked to significant words that were linguistically "feminine" in gender in the original lexicon of the church (Aramaic/Syriac, Hebrew, Greek, and Latin): words such as *wisdom, spirit, church, soul*, and *earth*.[2] As "the Woman" and "Virgin Mother"

1. Adam of Perseigne, "Sermon 5," 152.

2. See my book *The Woman, the Hour, and the Garden*, 27–39, for a discussion of "The 'Virgin Mother' in Christian Typology." I also recommend the intriguing scholarly speculations of Margaret Barker, which exhibit her thorough knowledge of the Old Testament and OT pseudepigrapha, the Dead Sea Scrolls, the New Testament and NT apocrypha (including the Nag Hammadi texts), patristic writings, and other relevant literature. She has much to say of value regarding "the Mother of the Lord" in her numerous studies of Temple worship. One can find a list of her books, as well as downloadable papers and other materials, on her website: http://www.margaretbarker.com/index.html.

of the Lord, she was from the earliest period viewed as the image and type of these "feminine" associations. She was seen also as the new Eve, "the mother of the living," and a type of "the virgin daughter of Zion" and the heavenly "Woman clothed with the sun" (see Revelation 12). In short, in Mary early Christians and subsequent generations recognized much more than a simple young woman from Nazareth chosen by God to give birth to Jesus. She was, from the church's beginnings, an increasingly multivalent figure. In the cited passage above, Adam of Perseigne lists three interpretations of "the valiant woman" of Proverbs 31, with whom he associates Mary: "the wisdom of God," "the church," and "the soul." In doing so, he reflects the first Christian millennium's perception of Mary's figurative meaning.

These three associations are interrelated, as Adam's sermon suggests. First, Mary was as an image or icon of *the church*—representative of the whole community of God's people. The roots of this image can be traced to the Old Testament's ascription of "virgin bride" to the holy city, Jerusalem/Zion, and to "her" as the "mother" of God's children. The prophetic books use the feminine metaphor repeatedly (e.g., Isa 49:18–23; 54:1–8; 66:7–14; Jer 2:1–3; Ezek 16:6–14; Hos 2:14–20). And the inclusion into the canon of the Song of Solomon was based on the rabbinical view that it was truly and mystically about Israel's loving bond with Yahweh.

The nuptial metaphor continues right into the New Testament writings to describe the people of God. For example, we find St. Paul reminding the church in Corinth that he had betrothed them "as a chaste virgin to Christ" (2 Cor 11:2). Elsewhere he describes the mystical "Jerusalem above" as "the mother of us all" (Gal 4:26); and—combining these two texts—the early church (*ekklesia*—feminine in gender) understood "herself" precisely as that mystical "Virgin Mother." The church, it was said, was a "virgin" when it kept the faith inviolate; it was a "mother" in bringing many children to new birth from her baptismal womb. We find nuptial imagery in the Gospels, as well. Jesus had posed the question to those disturbed by the fact that he and his disciples were not fasting at a time when it was expected that they should, "Can the wedding guests fast while the bridegroom is with them? As long as they have the bridegroom with them, they cannot fast" (Mark 2:19). By "bridegroom" he was indicating himself, and it seems evident that by "bride" he was designating the people of God. In the fourth Gospel, John the Baptist uses the same analogy to explain both his role and that of Jesus, describing himself as "the friend of the bridegroom": "He who has the bride is the bridegroom; the friend of the bridegroom, who stands and hears him, rejoices greatly at the bridegroom's voice" (John 3:29). The "bride" is the betrothed community that will bring many souls to new birth (a theme, of course, that is presented earlier in the same chapter).[3]

Countless texts in patristic and medieval sources compare the "Virgin Mother" church to the "Virgin Mother" Mary. It was simply a given to the early Christian mind that the two were reflective of one another. In the words of Hugo Rahner, "[E]verything that we find in the Gospel about Mary can be understood in a proper biblical sense of the mystery of the Church."[4] Just as Mary had virginally conceived and given birth to the physical body of Jesus, so the church conceived and gave new birth to the living members of the ecclesiastical "body" of Christ. As I have written elsewhere:

> [There is] no clear distinction . . . between the heavenly Israel/Jerusalem as "mother" of Jesus and the church as the "mother" of Jesus' disciples. There is only one "mother" and one archetypal "woman." Because of this long-ingrained idea, Augustine (354–430) could write, in a passage about the virgin mother Mary: "[T]he Church is the mother of Christ" [*Sermo Denis* 25,8].[5]
>
> [Mary] is thus the preeminent image of the church (the *qahal*, the *ekklesia*, the assembly of God's elect) that began with the "yes" of Abraham (Genesis 12), the church that experienced her betrothal at the foot of Mount Sinai, and had (as Origen put it in his *Commentary on the Song of Songs*) the Old Testament prophets, culminating with John the Baptist, as "friends of the Bridegroom," who had prepared her for her marriage to the Incarnate Word. "The wife of Christ" ("the wife of the Lamb"—Rev. 21:9), wherever such a notion is present in ancient Christian literature and imagery, both orthodox and heterodox, is therefore never to be taken literally; from the outset the idea is iconographic in nature only, a

3. As an aside, we must not be troubled by the fact that the image of Mary, identified as it was with the church, was fluid enough to encompass both the analogies of Christ's "bride" and "mother." This did not bother earlier generations of Christians, who understood well the poetic and spiritual nature of such imagery. Later generations of Christians have all too often—to their detriment—been literalists, whereas earlier generations were comfortable with allegory, multivalent types, and metaphor. They knew that these images pointed to realities otherwise impossible to articulate.

4. Rahner, *Our Lady and the Church*, 13.

5. Hart, *The Woman, the Hour, and the Garden*, 32.

> metaphor, a spiritual depiction of the loving relationship between Christ and the gathered community.[6]

The other two associations alluded to in the sermon of Adam of Perseigne—"wisdom" and the human "soul" (meaning, in this case, the comprehensive nature of a person, even to one's least consciously accessible inner depths)—can be taken together, as they relate both to the image of Mary and to each one of us, and by extension to the role of Mary in the mysteries of the rosary. Again, I quote from my earlier book:

> Mary was also at times . . . associated with the Old Testament personification of Wisdom [as was, of course, Christ]. It is the "wise" person [or soul], after all, who *receives* the implantation of God's Word, and every Christian is called to be a wise disciple (and thus a true "child" of the virgin mother church). One can see why Origen would mention her in relation to taking in the "wisdom" contained in the Gospel of John: "No one can apprehend the meaning of it except he have lain on Jesus' breast and received from Jesus Mary to be his mother also."[7]
>
> . . . Mary is aptly an image of the "wise soul," the wise disciple who gives birth to Christ within her. In this way she not only represents the community of faith, but also the faithful member of that community. The twelfth-century Cistercian Father Isaac of Stella, picking up this slim patristic thread, could thus write: "Whatever is said of God's eternal wisdom itself, can be applied in a wide sense to the Church, in a narrower sense to Mary, and in a particular way to every faithful soul."[8]

And, with the contemplative nature of the mysteries of the rosary particularly in mind here, the following passage indicates why Mary was from the church's beginning the symbol par excellence of the wise Christian disciple:

> Mary's wisdom was, of course, plainly visible in the biblical account. She had "kept all these things and pondered them in her heart . . . his mother kept all these things in her heart" (Luke 2:19, 51). She was, then, an icon of holy wisdom, pondering the mysteries of revelation. It was never lost on the mind of the church, visible in art and devotion throughout the Christian centuries,

6. Hart, *The Woman, the Hour, and the Garden*, 34.

7. Origen, *Commentary on the Gospel of John*, Bk. I, Ch. 6, 300.

8. Isaac of Stella, *Sermo 51*, on the Assumption, cited in Rahner, *Our Lady and the Church*.

> that Mary had conceived Jesus within her through her willing reception of the Word of God at the Annunciation. "Mary kept the words of Christ in her heart," wrote Origen, "kept them as a treasure, knowing that the time would come, when all that was hidden within her would be unveiled."[9] In a lesser way, as many of the Fathers—prominent among them Gregory Nazianzen and Gregory of Nyssa—asserted, Christ is conceived in our souls and so is born within us. Ambrose of Milan could say, for instance: "When the soul then begins to turn to Christ, she is addressed as 'Mary,' that is, she receives the name of the woman who bore Christ in her womb: for she has become a soul who in a spiritual sense gives birth to Christ."[10] In the words of Augustine: "When you look with wonder on what happened to Mary, you must imitate her in the depths of your own souls. Whoever believes with all his heart and is 'justified by faith' (Rom. 5:1), he has conceived Christ in the womb; and 'whenever with the mouth confession is made unto salvation' (Rom. 10:10), that man has given birth to Christ."[11, 12]

There can be little doubt, then, that the practice of praying the rosary, with its many repetitions of the *Ave Maria*, while simultaneously meditating on mysteries drawn from the accounts of Christ's life in order to "keep them and ponder them" in one's heart, had this rationale from the start. That the mysteries begin and end with the Virgin Mother alerts us to the fact that her multivalent image is set before our eyes as both the icon of the community of Christ, in which Mary's generation of Christ is perpetually reflected in the regeneration of his members, and the icon of the contemplative "wise soul," in whose heart Christ is born and abides.

So, we might say, that what Mary says to the angel, "Behold [*idou*] the handmaid of the Lord" (Luke 1:38), she is also saying to us who are attentive to the mysteries of Christ. "Behold" is a particularly important biblical word, and *beholding* is precisely what *we* are called to do before all else. As we behold her and the mysteries to which she points us in our silent meditation, we find ourselves looking into the depths of our own souls where, so we are assured, the Spirit of the Lord is at work.

9. Origen, *Homily on Luke*, 20, cited in Rahner, *Our Lady and the Church*.

10. Ambrose of Milan, *De Virginitate*, 4, 20, cited in Rahner, *Our Lady and the Church*.

11. Augustine, *Sermo 191*, 4, cited in Rahner, *Our Lady and the Church*.

12. For the two passages quoted above, see Hart, *The Woman, the Hour, and the Garden*, 34–37.

Beholding and Iconography

Throughout her masterly two-volume work on the place of silence in classical Christian spiritual practice, *Silence: A User's Guide*, Maggie Ross argues that the English word *behold* is still the best word to use when translating Hebrew and Greek equivalents for English versions of the Bible. I believe she makes a good case on lexical and other grounds, and I refer readers to her books to weigh her arguments for themselves. In this section, I cite only a few of her comments that I think particularly relevant to the topic at hand. In the final chapter of her work, then, she writes:

> The word *behold* is arguably the most important word in the Bible and by extension in spiritual life, which it epitomizes, and its significance is transmitted through the early history of Christianity into the Middle Ages . . . Despite . . . the word's centrality to the biblical text, it has been dropped from most modern translations of the Bible, changing and draining the essential meaning and theology of many passages, and negatively affecting the modern interpretation of medieval texts.

She continues with an explanation of why she prefers to use *behold* rather than other words that have been used in various translations (such as "look," "remember," and even "in fact") when a translation has not dropped the word altogether:

> The English word *behold* accurately conveys the many psychological and theological nuances of both Hebrew (*hinneh*) and Greek (*idou, theoreo*) from which it is translated . . .

> "Behold" is a word that alerts us to pause, however briefly, to be vigilant, because something new, something startling, is about to be revealed. Beholding is a process of continual death (the mind being temporarily brought to silence) and resurrection (the arrival of a new perspective).[1]

We need to pause and take in her point. To be entreated to "behold" something, in the insistent sense that the biblical literature intends that word to be received, is to be urged to do more than simply to look at something. Nor is it merely a request to "pay attention" to something. The significance of the word includes "paying attention," but it frequently points one beyond what we think of as intellectual comprehension (to "comprehend" means to "encompass" or "contain"), because it confronts the one who is exhorted to "behold" with the unanticipated and obscure. When one is told or beseeched to "behold" in Scripture, it is not in order to present that person with an "idea" to be "grasped," but instead to present something that takes hold on the hearer and compels him or her to let go and be responsive. We can perhaps get a hint of this in such biblical texts as (to choose three out of hundreds): "*Behold*, I send my messenger to prepare the way before me" (Mal 3:1); "*Behold*, the Lamb of God, who takes away the sin of the world!" (John 1:29); and the second of the two selected texts that introduced this volume at the outset, and a text—as Maggie Ross reminds us—that has always been central to the contemplative tradition: "The kingdom of God is not coming with observation, nor will they say, '*Behold*—here it is,' or, 'There it is.' For *behold*—the kingdom of God is within you" (Luke 17:20b–21). "Beholding" elicits a gratuitous suspension of thought and a cessation of words, an awakening to, and an encounter with, that which goes beyond the ordinary state of awareness. It is to enter ("however briefly") into a "cloud of unknowing," stopping us in our mental tracks. It creates a liminal hiatus, an interruption, and a call to let go mentally. Even if that which is unexpectedly "beheld" is something that has been perceived many times before as ordinary, in the act of "beholding" it afresh that same ordinary thing can become—at least, for the moment—"new" and extraordinary to one's perceptions.

An example of what "beholding" means for the beholder can be glimpsed in another faith tradition, in what we see expressed in the poetry of Ch'an or Zen Buddhism. Randomly opening a small collection that I

1. Ross, *Silence (Volume 2)*, 129.

have here on my desk as I write, for instance, I read a poem of Hanshan (or "Cold Mountain," eighth century, Chinese), translated by Robert Henricks:

> My mind is like the autumn moon
> An emerald lake—pure, clean and bright.
>
> There is nothing with which it compares;
> Tell me, how can I explain?[2]

This poem expresses beholding very well and its effect on one's thinking: "Tell me, how can I explain?" Hanshan is responding to the sight of the autumn moon and the emerald lake, and there can be no doubt that something in these natural sights have awakened in him an awareness that goes beyond words. Zen never tries to describe, but only to point to an encounter that cannot be directly shared.

Here is another poem from the same collection, selected at random, this one by Saigyo (1118–1190, Japanese), and translated by Geoffrey Bownas and Anthony Thwaite:

> The winds of spring
> Scattered the flowers
> As I dreamt my dream.
> Now I awaken,
> My heart is disturbed.[3]

Again, we have—as is common in such poetry—an allusion to a natural sight, in this case flowers scattered by spring winds. There is an "awakening" and a "disturbance" in the poet's heart. How are we to understand that? Once more, it is a suggestion that a "beholding" has occurred, something extraordinary in the very ordinary sight of blown flowers that interrupted the poet's dreaming, pulling him—newly aware—out of his reveries. If one misses such allusions in Zen poetry, one misses the point entirely. At any rate, what is indicated is a fresh "seeing" that goes beyond what is seen physically, on the surface of things—an "awakening" indeed. There is an abrupt pause in one's normal perception, as one is charged by a wholly new perception.

This sort of occurrence finds its counterpart, as many have noted for some decades, in classical Christian meditation. Maggie Ross's assertion

2. Harris, *Zen Poems*, 71.

3. Harris, *Zen Poems*, 126.

quoted above, that "[b]eholding is a process of continual death (the mind being temporarily brought to silence) and resurrection (the arrival of a new perspective)," could with no real difficulty be transposed to the Zen context. Zen poetry about awakening is most often connected to engagement with the natural world (and this is something that Christians, whose religion is centered on belief in the incarnation of the Word and the Father "who is above all and through all and in all" [Eph 4:6] should easily embrace), but the fruit of Zen practice also finds expression in the art of painting (as it also does in Taoism, which greatly influenced Ch'an in China). For example, the famous "Ox Herder" series of pictures function in a somewhat similar fashion to how Christian iconography does in its context.[4] The art is meant to sweep the mind into an altered view of what is depicted, so that the *essence* of it is appreciated. The underlying essence in Zen art is "emptiness," the dynamic ground from which all that exists springs forth incessantly. Comparatively speaking, the underlying essence in classical Christian iconography is the "uncreated light" or "glory" of the divine—in other words, it is a radically "transfigured" depiction of a person or event (and, in this feature, it differs from the nature-inspired art of Zen Buddhism and Taoism).

This book, of course, is a gallery of Christian iconography, and so a few words need to be said about how this art is connected to what we have already said about "beholding." Solrunn Nes has explained the formal and classical characteristics that demarcate her art in her book *The Mystical Language of Icons*, and I would direct the reader to that beautifully illustrated work for a more thorough look at the art.[5] But I shall draw from it here to point out how the art in this book might "work" to move the viewer toward "beholding." Among the characteristics of iconography that she notes are its "inconsistent perspective," "inverse perspective," "hierarchical perspective," and icons' presentation of light. About "inconsistent perspective," she writes:

> Elements such as the surroundings and architecture [in the painted image of a given icon], which contribute to the environment [as depicted in it], function as scenery for the person or event [that is the focus of the motif], and a building is often seen from different angles at the same time. This *inconsistent perspective* gives the

4. See my book on the "Ox Herder" series of ten pictures, *The Ox-Herder and the Good Shepherd*.

5. Nes, *The Mystical Language of Icons*.

> elements a flat quality and counteracts the illusion of depth. The object is not to give a realistic impression; on the contrary, it is to lead the thoughts towards an existence that is "without end."

We might say, in other words, that this is intended to reveal that the infinite is always the background of the finite, and that the eternal is present within and beyond the event or person shown. Again, in the words of Ephesians 4:6, it is an indication of the presence of the invisible Father "who is above all and through all and in all."

Solrunn continues by describing the closely related use of "inverse perspective":

> To show that the icon refers to a transcendent dimension, *inverse perspective* is used. This is done by making the objects farthest away the largest and the closest ones smallest. Following this principle, a rectangular footstool would be depicted as smaller at the front than at the back. The sloping lines on each side (the orthogonals) do not converge towards a vanishing point on the surface of the icon as they do in a naturalistic painting, but diverge into infinite space "behind" the motif. If we follow the lines in the opposite direction, we find that they meet at the spectator. It is as if the spectator is being looked at by the person in the portrait.

There are no iconic "portraits" in this book, and so the inverse perspective is not much in evidence here. But, that said, we are reminded that the purpose of the icon is to create within the viewer an unusual perception of reality—in this case, that the art is addressing her or him, that it is observing *us* and, in some sense, made to appear that it is examining the thoughts of our hearts.

"Hierarchical perspective" is addressed next by Solrunn:

> Another special feature of icons is that when compared to the surroundings the main figure is often strikingly large. This is called *hierarchical perspective*. For example, a motif of the Nativity [in this book, it is the third motif presented] shows Mary resting on a covering in the centre of the painting while the Child Jesus, who appears unnaturally large for a newly-born baby, lies in a crib painted in inverse perspective. The other people in the composition—Joseph, the shepherds and the women who washed Jesus—are secondary and accordingly relatively small compared to the Mother of God and the Child Jesus.

The simple point that this perspective makes, of course, is to identify those who are the most significant figures in a given scene. What we should take away from this is that, once again, iconography is not "religious art" in the sense of depicting a biblical (or other) motif as the artist imagines it might *actually have looked*. It is, rather, symbolic art, quite intentionally defying all rules of naturalism, not merely to avoid any semblance of idolatry, but to alert the viewer that he or she is meant to *see through* the art towards that which is indefinable. In other words, by virtue of its anti-realism, it is—as with the biblical sense of "beholding"—meant to silence us and bring us up short in all our ordinary expectations of what art is "supposed" to do. It is an invitation to death (of our suppositions) and resurrection (a renewed vision).

Lastly, Solrunn focuses on how light is depicted, even simulated, within the icon:

> Light . . . radiates from the motif itself, and not, as is the case in a realistic painting, from a conjectured exterior source of light. Of course, there is no sharply outlined shadow on the icon, only a certain degree of object shadow. The face, robes, hills and buildings are modelled by giving them lighter or darker shades of the local colour . . . The [depiction of material reality] is no longer solid, but permeable and transparent, with the ability to reflect the rays from a divine source of light.

What the "light" within an icon is intended to evoke is that "light" and "glory" mentioned in 2 Corinthians 3:18 and 4:6, cited at the outset of this book: "But we all, with open face beholding as in a [mirror] the glory of the Lord, are changed into the same image from glory to glory, even as by the Spirit of the Lord . . . For God, who commanded the light to shine out of darkness, hath shined in our hearts, to give the light of the knowledge of the glory of God in the face of Jesus Christ" (2 Cor 3:18; 4:6 KJV). The word *changed* (*metamorphoumetha*—to undergo metamorphosis) is the same word used in the Gospels to describe Jesus' "transfiguration" on the mount. It is a reminder—as we will have occasion to note when we reach that particular mystery in the pages ahead—that we, and the whole of creation, are destined for "transfiguration" and the "restitution [*apokatastaseos*] of all things" (Acts 3:21 KJV).

Solrunn concludes her short excursion through the formal characteristics of iconographic art with these words:

> [The iconographic artistic] style . . . underlines its universality and timelessness. As an expression of divine revelation the icon is subject to neither the laws of nature nor the reason of man. The icon is thus no illusion of the physical, visible world, but a vision of the spiritual, invisible world.[6]

Although the style of the icon is designed to counter conventions of reason, it is certainly not an unreasonable form of art if one accepts it on its own terms. That is to say, it is intelligible with some grounding in age-old Christian symbolism and typology. It can be "read," in fact, like a text.

In the classical world that gave birth to Jewish, pagan, and Christian literature, it was common to distinguish between the "senses" of a written text. On the surface of any literature in question, regardless of the genre, was the "literal" sense. The literal sense meant only that which was "literally" set down on the page. It had nothing to do with whether or not what was written was factual or not; it had to do with *what was found in the text word by word*. So, for example, one could read *The Odyssey* of Homer "literally," even though no one would have regarded that great poem as a record of factual events. Beyond the literal sense, there were those other senses that pertained to *meaning*—arguably, the more important senses of a text. The ancient Greeks read *The Odyssey* not only as a literal story, but also as a great moral and allegorical epic. In Christianity, these same senses were distinguished as "literal" and "spiritual," and the latter sense was divided into three subsets: the *moral* sense, which had to do with guidance in living the Christian life justly, mercifully, and ethically; the *allegorical* sense, in which the symbols and types to be found in texts, including "historical" accounts, were interpreted in ways similar to how the imagery in the book of Revelation or parables of Jesus were also interpreted (to give one example, many early Christian exegetes—for instance, Origen—read the Gospels as an interweaving of historical detail and invented elements);[7] and, lastly, the *anagogical* ("uplifting" or "ascending") sense, which indicates how the text in question points the reader to his or her ultimate aim—"heaven," "the age to come," the great *Apokatastasis* ("Restoration"), and so on. It is this last sense, and also the moral sense, to which Paul refers, when he writes to the Romans, "For whatever was written in former days was written for our instruction, that by steadfastness and by the encouragement of the scriptures we might have hope" (Rom 15:4), and to the Corinthians: "Now

6. Nes, *The Mystical Language of Icons*. All the above quotes come from pp. 20–21.

7. See my *The Woman, the Hour, and the Garden*, 21–24.

these things happened [to the Israelites of the exodus] figuratively, and were written for the purpose of our admonition, for whom the ends of the ages have arrived" (1 Cor 10:11).[8]

This seeming digression is applicable when "reading" an icon (and also when "reading" a "mystery" of the rosary). In looking at an icon, one sees the style plainly enough, with its various perspectives as described above. One can be moved—or not—by this kind of art, and learn to distinguish between icons of greater and lesser quality. So, for example, one can be powerfully stirred by, say, the famous icon of the Trinity of Andrei Rublev (c. 1365–c. 1428), and yet still not have a clue what the various attributes, gestures, coloration, and other symbols *signify*. In the very first icon in this book, to take another example, which depicts the Annunciation, one will note that the Virgin holds in her hand a spindle of scarlet yarn (which will be explained in the accompanying text there). It is a seemingly insignificant—often going unnoticed—detail, but it is a very important one that should be noted. In other words, one can appreciate the "literal sense" of the artwork of an icon, but totally miss the "spiritual senses" that the icon points toward, which lie beyond the surface of the work (one wishes that biblical literalists understood something similar about the nature of the Bible when they read it). Throughout this book, we will endeavor to point out features in each icon that are meant to catch our attention and need some interpretation.

The icon and the mysteries of the rosary are inducements to fall silent, to look, to take in, and to go beyond. In our receptiveness, the possibility of truly "beholding"—which cannot be reduced to words or theories or rational articulation or "ideas"—can occur. When, in contemplation, this happens, it is felt as the partial letting go of a consuming sense of "self" or ego, and it is a work of grace. It is a jolt of reality, an awakening, and—in the familiar terms Christians employ—an encounter with the Holy Spirit. It cannot be "made to happen," but one can certainly prepare one's heart for such an occurrence. Contemplative prayer is a discipline and needs time to develop, but for those willing to practice, it is worth the effort. As aids to that endeavor, both iconography and the mysteries presented here can be useful.

8. D. B. Hart, *The New Testament*, 336.

Four Sets of Five

There are four essential concepts interwoven throughout the mysteries of the rosary. They can be classified as *incarnation*, *revelation*, *kenosis*, and *regeneration*.

The concept of Christ's *incarnation* finds its biblical basis most obviously in the "Prologue" of John's Gospel: "In the beginning was the Word [*logos*], and the Word was with God, and the Word was God . . . And the Word became flesh and dwelt among us" (John 1:1, 14). John also refers to the Word as "the Son" of God, an identification we also find outside the New Testament in both ancient Christian and non-Christian texts—for example, in the writings of the first-century Jewish philosopher and exegete, Philo. According to John, this divine person—the "Word" and "Son"—became "incarnate" (en-fleshed) in the man Jesus from Nazareth. In other words, in Jesus we encounter God in human form: "He who has seen me has seen the Father" (John 14:9).

The next term, *revelation*, is virtually self-explanatory. Through Jesus, God has made himself known in a way that human beings can recognize and relate to (though, of course, not entirely comprehend): "We have beheld his glory" (John 1:14). His miracles or "signs" (as John calls them), his teachings, his acts of compassion and forgiveness, his table fellowship (extended through the institution of the Lord's Supper), and more, were all means through which Jesus revealed—unveiled—the reality of God's gracious manifestation among human beings.

Kenosis, the third of our four classifications, is a word meaning to become "empty." Where Jesus is concerned, it indicates his "self-emptying" of divine status, even to the point of abasement and an ignominious death.

In other words, it goes quite a few steps further "down" than the concept of incarnation does. One could certainly conceive of an "incarnation" that did not entail the cross. The key text for the concept of Christ's *kenosis* is found in an important passage of Paul's Letter to the Philippians: "[Christ Jesus] emptied himself, taking the form of a servant [literally, slave]" (Phil 2:7). We will return to this crucial passage—"crucial" because it declares his death on the cross—since it has particular import for us (it pointedly follows the appeal, "Have this [same] mind in yourselves"). The self-emptying of Jesus is meant to be mirrored in our own emptying of "self," meaning the pouring out of our ego-centered prerogatives and off-kilter tendencies and more. Whereas *incarnation* referred to the eternal Word/Son "becoming man," *kenosis* refers to his loss of everything in the process—status, dignity, and life itself.

The fourth of our categories is *regeneration*, which literally means "rebirth." It is through our union with the death, resurrection, and glorification of Christ that our "rebirth" is realized. These significant acts of Christ are set before Christian disciples as the path we must all travel in the course of our lives and within our deepest selves. Baptism is "the outward and visible sign" of rebirth, our sacramental identification with Jesus' death, burial, resurrection, and ascension. So it is that Paul writes to the church in Rome: "Do you not know that all of us who have been baptized into Christ Jesus were baptized into his *death*? We were *buried* therefore with him by baptism into death, so that as Christ was *raised* from the dead by the glory of the Father, *we too* might walk in *newness of life*" (Rom 6:3–4; emphasis mine). The pattern of regeneration is made tangible to us through the act of baptism. It is also a call to ongoing transformation: "Baptism . . . now saves you . . . as an appeal to God for a clear conscience" (1 Pet 3:21). "Death" and "resurrection" characterize the lives we are to live as followers of Jesus. As Paul wrote to the Corinthians: "Therefore, if any one is in Christ, he is a new creation; the old has passed away, behold [*idou*], the new has come" (2 Cor 5:17). Death, resurrection, and the *ascension*, as well, are not simply events that occurred in time "out there," but are realities internal to us. The Pauline Letter to the Colossians puts it this way: "If then you have been raised with Christ, seek the things that are above, where Christ is, seated at the right hand of God. Set your minds on things above, where Christ is, seated at the right hand of God" (Col 3:1–2). As paradoxical as it might sound, we "set our minds on things above" by a continuing practice of "going into our room"—that is, into our interior or "deep mind," to borrow

Maggie Ross's phrase—"and shutting the door and praying to our Father who is in secret" (see Matt 6:6). Regeneration is a lifetime's work in progress within the depths of our "hearts."

All four of these concepts—incarnation, revelation, kenosis, and regeneration—are inseparable; you cannot find one without finding the rest as well. And this can be seen in the four sets of five mysteries that together make up the rosary's full round of twenty. Each set—going under the customary headings of "Joyful," "Luminous," "Sorrowful," and "Glorious" respectively—emphasizes one of the four concepts presented above, but the other concepts are never absent, no matter which one is the focus of a given set.

Here, then, are the four sets. With each I have specified the concept, from the classifications above, that is the chief focus for each:

The "Joyful" Mysteries—highlighting *incarnation*:

The Annunciation to Mary

The Visitation of Mary to Elizabeth

The Nativity of Jesus

The Presentation of Jesus in the Temple

The Finding of Jesus in the Temple at Age Twelve

The "Luminous" Mysteries—highlighting *revelation*:

The Baptism of Jesus

The Wedding Feast at Cana

Jesus' Teaching about the Kingdom of God

Jesus' Transfiguration on the Mountain

The Institution of the Lord's Supper

The "Sorrowful" Mysteries—highlighting *kenosis*:

Jesus in the Garden of Gethsemane

The Scourging of Jesus

Jesus is Crowned with Thorns

The Carrying of the Cross

Jesus' Crucifixion and Death

The "Glorious" Mysteries—highlighting *regeneration*:

The Resurrection of Christ

The Ascension of Christ

The Descent of the Spirit

The Assumption of Mary

The Coronation of Mary

There are a variety of customs that have attached themselves, as the tradition has developed, to meditation on the mysteries. The most common is the assigning of one set of five to specific days of the week. Such customs do not concern us in this book, since this is a book of iconography suitable for meditation above all else. As I have indicated above, the sort of meditation I think most beneficial is silent and contemplative in nature. It is a much older form of Christian meditation, with roots in the great contemplative tradition we find in, for example, the Desert Fathers and Mothers, the Cappadocian saints—both male and female, Evagrios of Pontus, John Cassian, Dionysius the Areopagite, Isaac of Syria, the great Carthusian and Cistercian writers of the twelfth and thirteenth centuries, Richard of St. Victor, Jan van Ruysbroeck, Meister Eckhart and Johannes Tauler, Nicholas of Cusa, the author of *The Cloud of Unknowing*, Dame Julian of Norwich, Marguerite Porete, and so on (the list is long). In our own day, we can add the names of Thomas Merton, Bede Griffiths, John Main, and others. The ancient practice of silent prayer is neither difficult nor dangerous. It is rarely taught, however, and that is something else entirely. Indeed, it is quite simple to do, and it is mercifully devoid of such intrusive—even if well-intentioned—devotional impositions and complications as moralism, demands to "reflect" on abstract "virtues," imaginative visualizing, the unfortunate piling up of verbal prayers, and any insistence that the meditator endeavor to summon up "appropriate" feelings (this last being the reason I tend to be uneasy using the terms "joyful" and "sorrowful" for the first and third sets of mysteries). Anyone with a mind to do so, in other words, can learn to practice the prayer of silence.

As a method for meditation on the mysteries, I would suggest focusing on just one mystery at a time, rather than five, with or without rosary in hand, with or without words of any kind. The icons in this book are suited for precisely that kind of slow, relaxed, non-verbal contemplative practice. If one wishes to use the beads, one might use them beforehand as a preparation for focusing the gaze and the mind. But, then, one would do well to foster a daily practice of stillness and silence (as the great Desert Father, Abba Moses the Black advised one seeker, "Go, sit in your cell, and your cell will teach you everything"). The goal, in this case, is to let the mysteries speak to us in their own silent way, without inner or outer distraction. We should not be bringing our own ideas to them but allowing them to work on our quietened minds. Neither should we try to conjure in ourselves what we think "should" be the "right" feelings. The icons are there in order to be reflected in the "mirror" of our still minds, and we should be prepared—should we undergo a moment of "beholding"—to pass beyond them into an imageless, wordless encounter.

The "shape" the order of the sequence of mysteries takes and that of our spiritual lives are analogous: both descend and ascend. As Maggie Ross explains, when describing the inner work of silent prayer:

> What I'm trying to say here is very simple: life, transfiguration, death, and resurrection—all are to be found in the work of silence, particularly as it is laid out in the kenotic hymn (Phil 2:5–11). This is why Jesus is both the paradigm and parable of silence. This is why for Christians the work of silence may be understood as the en-Christing process: Christ is a way of knowing; Christ is a way of being in the community that is the world; Christ is wisdom; Christ is the way of doing theology. Christ is beholding: behold, and all the rest shall be added unto you.[1]

Here, then, is the kenotic hymn from Paul's Letter to the Philippians, the importance of which Ross stresses and to which I have also referred. Possibly this text was originally part of an ancient liturgy, from which Paul borrowed, or perhaps it was his own composition. Either way, it appears in his letter precisely to provide for his readers a paradigm for the life lived in Christ. Note the descent-ascent "shape" of it:

> Have this mind among yourselves, which is yours in Christ Jesus, who, though he was in the form of God, did not count equality with God a thing to be grasped, but emptied himself, taking the form of a servant, being born in the likeness of men. And being found in human form he humbled himself and became obedient unto death, even death on a cross. Therefore God has highly exalted him and bestowed on him the name which is above every name, that at the name of Jesus every knee should bow, in heaven and on earth and under the earth, and every tongue confess that Jesus Christ is Lord, to the glory of God the Father. (Phil 2:5–11)

1. Ross, *Silence (Volume 1)*, 222.

So it is that Paul gives us an understanding of discipleship as Christ-shaped and Christ-centered. If the one who shared divine status with the Father "emptied himself" of status, privilege, glory, and even his essential human worth ("even death on a cross" implied exactly that in the ancient world), what can it be that his followers are meant to do when they "take up the cross" themselves? This is not a question of our outward physical martyrdom (which the great majority of Christians have never undergone), but, what is much more common, of our inward consciousness—"be of *that mind in yourselves*." *We* are called to realize that what we call our "selves" or our "identities" are mutable and ephemeral, that when we come to die we will leave behind whatever we are now and become something new. This is not a matter of leaving behind a "false self" in order to discover our "authentic self"—Christian spirituality is no more a program for "discovering our selves" than Buddhism is. Rather, it is letting go of our selves in the silence of God and discovering that "in [God] we live and move and have our being" (Acts 17:28). For us, that is the first direct intimation of resurrection, and it happens *within* us—"for behold— the kingdom of God is within you" (Luke 17:21). It is toward *this* pattern of our existence that the mysteries of the rosary point us.

So, in the gallery we are about to enter we behold Mary, that perennial image of wisdom and our receptive souls. With her, we are ready to ponder all these things in our hearts. We will look at selected mysteries of Jesus' descent and ascent, and perhaps through them see our own. Beyond these images, we desire to encounter the silence of communion with God in meditation. That is the hope, at any rate, which the author and artist share for the readers of this book.

Part Two

The Twenty Mysteries

For each of the twenty icons that follow, I have provided a commentary. And in each of these commentaries, which vary in length, I have set out to include the following features.

First, at some point in every commentary I point out a few key elements pictured in each image in order to highlight what they symbolize or suggest. I have not tried to be exhaustive in this endeavor and, as a matter of principle, have left a number of items to the viewer's own perceptions and interpretation. Every person will, I hope, discover aspects for themselves that "speak" in a special way to her or him.

For each of the mysteries, I have also offered a list of recommended texts (mostly biblical) for readers to look up on their own. Those who practice the age-old tradition of *lectio divina*—"holy reading"—may find these useful as they reflect on the images. I have also commented on the relevant texts, and in so doing I have adhered to what I hold to be sound principles of modern exegesis and literary analysis. Again, these are not exhaustive treatments of the texts, but neither are they what can be called "devotional" readings. My approach is not an "affective" one. In other words, there has been no effort on my part to stir up pious feelings in the reader, but rather meditative reflectiveness.

I have also written for readers who are, I trust, familiar with contemporary biblical research and who do not fear it as a threat to their faith, even if at times it poses challenges to literalism and not a few fond and even "traditional" misconceptions. Readers will quickly ascertain, for example, that I do not affirm the thoroughly untenable position that the Bible is internally "non-contradictory" in nature. The Bible is a great library, spanning in its composition hundreds of years, made up of many genres, and involving many different perspectives. It has no single religious perspective, and there are even competing views gathered within its carefully edited and reedited pages. In this book, given the subject matter, it is the New Testament that gets most attention. And there, as with the Old Testament, one will not find internal conformity, but a diversity of views held together in the embrace of a uniting faith. There is nothing discouraging in that fact. It is often out of the striking differences that, in truth, exist between Gospel and Gospel and Scripture-writer and Scripture-writer that profound insights can emerge.

Lastly, one important aspect of these commentaries has been to present some thoughts on the "spiritual sense" of each mystery (see Section 4 of the First Part above)—highlighting how each mystery might influence our lives of prayer and also, in general terms, our social awareness and action. Prayer and action are intimately connected to one another in Christian discipleship, and this will be a recurring focus in the commentaries that follow.

First Set: The "Joyful" Mysteries

Incarnation

The First Mystery

The Annunciation to Mary

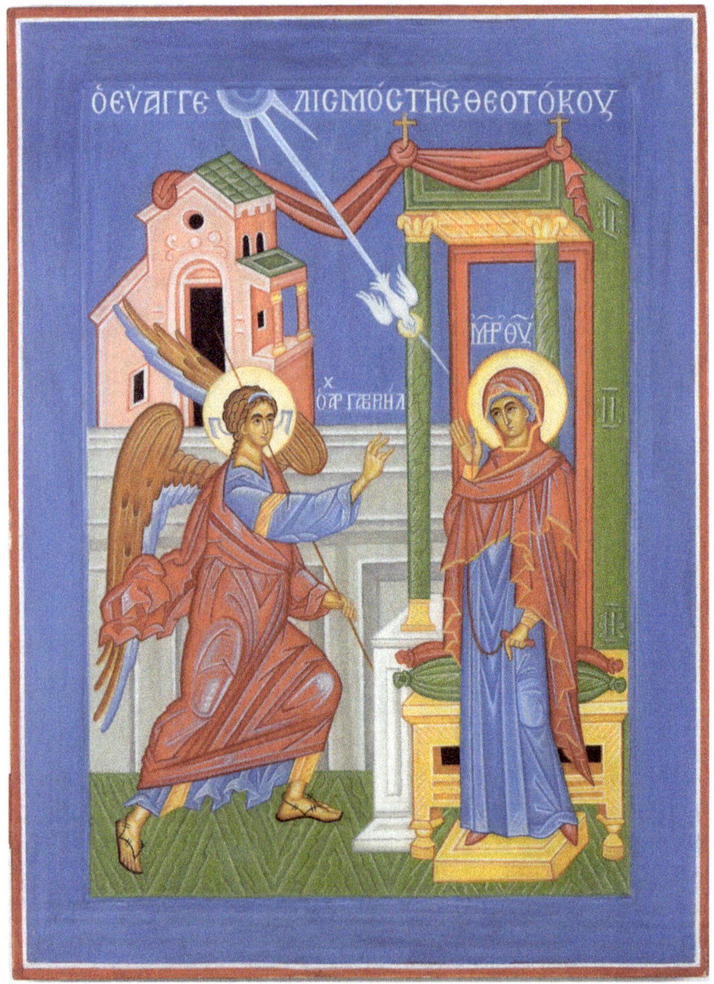

Readings for reflection:

> Luke 1:26-38; *The Protevangelium (Infancy Gospel) of James* (2nd/3rd century), Chapters 7–11[1]

1. There are many English versions of this ancient apocryphal work, both in print and online. A fine, easily readable translation can be found in Margaret Barker's *Christmas*, 128–61, along with her fascinating commentary on the text. Another, older, and

The Annunciation is not only the first in the series of mysteries, but it can be said to contain all the rest. That is to say, it is the mystery that is the source, the fountainhead, from which all the others flow. Its iconographic complement will be reached in the twentieth and final mystery, the Coronation of Mary, which will bring the entire series full circle.

The significance of the Annunciation is reflected in our icon, which is rich in traditional detail and symbols. In the scene we have before us, a young woman stands face to face with a mysterious stranger, an angel. To early Christians, this tableau had correlations with the third chapter of Genesis, in which Eve consents to take what is offered to her by another mysterious being. In Eve's case, her thoughts are sown with the seed of a suggestion that "that ancient serpent who is called the Devil and Satan" (Rev 12:9) plants. Eve is lured to take the deadly fruit; Mary is invited to receive the life-giving Lord to become the fruit of her womb.

By the time Irenaeus of Lyons was writing in the second century, it was already customary to regard Mary as "the new Eve," the new "mother of all the living," and her assent to God's word as undoing Eve's assent to the serpent's enticement. Irenaeus was merely stating this established belief when he wrote: "Adam had to be recapitulated in Christ so that mortality might be swallowed up in immortality (1 Corinthians 15.53; 2 Corinthians 5.4). Eve had to be recapitulated in Mary so that a virgin would be the intercessor for a virgin, and by the obedience of a virgin, undo and overcome the disobedience of a virgin."[2] Latin hymnographers, carrying on the same theme in later times, were given to whimsical wordplay when they made Gabriel's *Ave* an inversion of the name *Eva.* The story of the Annunciation, seen in this light, was an image of hope for earthly creation and for the restoration of the human race.

---

scholarly version, useful for its introductory notes by Oscar Cullmann, can be found in Hennecke, *New Testament Apocrypha*, 363–88.

Regarding the *Protevangelium*, Barker makes a point that deserves consideration, especially as we look at the iconography of these first few mysteries, incorporating as they do elements taken from that work, which are not to be found in the canonical Gospels: "Scholars used to assume that the *Protevangelium* was just a fanciful elaboration of the stories in Matthew and Luke, but opinion is now changing. It may have drawn on the same sources as did Matthew and Luke, but it used more of them and in its own way . . . 'The stories that came to make up the *Protevangelium* and its companion gospels seem to have been a part of the life of the church during the first generations'" (Barker, *Christmas*, 130; her citation comes from Cartlidge and Elliott, *Art and the Christian Apocrypha*, 23).

2. Irenaios, *The Preaching of the Apostles*, (ch. 32), 48.

Mary's visitor, the heavenly messenger Gabriel, had appeared in the Old Testament book of Daniel (as well as in intertestamental literature). There he was depicted as a revealer of mysteries pertaining to the final events of history (Dan 8:15–19; 9:20–23). That it is Gabriel who comes to Mary in the story of the Annunciation indicates that the time of history's fulfillment has arrived. That it is Mary to whom he comes, however, tells us that the manner of this fulfillment is not to be one of general unveiling—there will be no astounding cosmic signs manifested before the eyes of the world, nothing sensational in nature. Rather, the Messiah comes unexpectedly, silently, and invisibly. This theme of a "hidden descent" of Christ was, in fact, an early feature of Christian belief. Among the more notable figures who mentioned it was Ignatius of Antioch (d. circa 110), whose own letters nearly made it into the New Testament: "Mary's virginity was hidden from the prince of this world; so was her childbearing, and so was the death of the Lord."[3] Similarly, Irenaeus wrote: "Since the Word descended invisible to creatures, He was not known to them in that act."[4] The idea of the hidden descent may have derived from Wisdom 18:14–15, a text still used in the Christmas liturgy: "For while gentle silence enveloped all things . . . thy all-powerful word leaped from heaven, from the royal throne . . . and touched heaven while standing on the earth." But it may also derive from an authentic detail, picked up in the Gospel of John, that Jesus' Galilean background was confusing to many of his hearers: "'Yet we know where this man comes from; and when the Christ appears, no one will know where he comes from' . . . But [others] said, 'Is the Christ to come from Galilee? Has not the scripture said that the Christ is descended from David, and comes from Bethlehem, the village where David was?'" (John 7:27, 41b–42). When Jesus appeared, his origins were apparently obscure to many.

The context we see depicted in the icon is the home of Mary, but the story connects the scene to the Temple in Jerusalem. How can we know this? Because Mary is holding a spindle of thread in her hand as the angel addresses her. This small but significant detail is not to be found in Luke's Gospel, but rather in *The Protevangelium of James*. The latter is a very early apocryphal work that has exercised considerable influence in the traditional picture of the events surrounding Jesus' birth. If we bear in mind that neither iconography nor the mysteries of the rosary put the stress on literal history (which is not possible to reconstruct with precision anyway),

3. Ignatius of Antioch, *Letter to the Ephesians*, 19.

4. Irenaios, *The Preaching of the Apostles*, (ch. 83), 81.

we will be better prepared to "read" the meaning we see in this and the other icons. The context shown in the Annunciation icon, then, has direct associations with the Temple, and with the Temple veil in particular, and this detail comes from the *Protevangelium*.

As a child, according to the *Protevangelium*, Mary's parents take her to be raised in the Temple until she is of marriageable age, because of a promise they had made to the Lord. Typologically, the Temple and the Ark of the Covenant are both related to the image of Mary in Christian tradition. She "houses" the Son of God in herself, as the Temple "houses" God's presence on earth. But this is not what the *Protevangelium* seems to be emphasizing. Rather, it appears to present her as the earthly image of the heavenly "Lady" Wisdom, whose earthly abode—according to Jewish tradition—was the Temple.[5] For instance, Wisdom—always feminine in gender—says of herself in the book of Sirach: "In the holy tabernacle I ministered before him and so I was established in Zion. In the beloved city likewise he gave me a resting place, and in Jerusalem was my dominion" (Sir 24:10–11). The description of the playful Wisdom of the book of Proverbs is also taken up in the *Protevangelium*. In Proverbs, we hear Wisdom say: "I was daily [the LORD's] delight, rejoicing before him always, rejoicing in his inhabited world and delighting in the sons of men" (Prov 8:30b–31). Of the little girl Mary, the *Protevangelium* says that "the Lord put grace on her and she danced with her feet and all the house of Israel loved her" (*Prot.*, 7). The Jewish philosopher and exegete Philo, the contemporary of Jesus, was picking up on the lengthy monologue of Wisdom in Proverbs 8 when he referred to Wisdom as "the first-born mother of all things."[6] Not only is Mary, then, the counterpart to Eve, "the mother of all the living," but also the earthly representation of Wisdom, "the mother of all things." By receiving Christ into her womb, Mary becomes the mother of the new creation.

5. It is a common feature of Hebrew and Jewish-Christian typology that heavenly realities have their earthly representations. To provide one Christian canonical text as an example of this essential feature, picked from among many, here is Hebrews 8:5: "[The Jerusalem Temple priests] serve as a copy and shadow of the heavenly sanctuary; for when Moses was about to erect the tent, he was instructed by God, saying, 'See that you make everything according to the pattern which was shown you on the mountain'" (cf. Exod 25:40). This typological principle applies as well to such figures as Mary. For instance, Mary is the earthly counterpart of the "woman clothed with the sun" (who is Wisdom, Spirit, the community of the elect, the Bride of the Lamb, and the New Jerusalem rolled into one)—who is also associated with the Ark in the heavenly Temple—in Revelation 11:19—12:17.

6. Quoted in Barker, *Christmas*, 141.

None of this symbolism, it must be stressed, would have surprised early Christians, even if it seems strange to us in our age of shriveled mythopoeic sensibilities.

Which brings us back to the spindle of thread that Mary holds in her hand in the icon. The *Protevangelium* gives us the key to understanding the symbolism. "The priests held a council," it says, "and [they] said: 'Let us make a new veil for the Temple of the Lord.'" Lots are cast to determine which of the seven "pure virgins of Israel" summoned for the task will contribute to the weaving of the veil. "The lots for the true purple and the scarlet [threads] fell to Mary, and she took them home" (*Prot.*, 7). At home, she first hears the angel address her as she is drawing water from the well. Frightened, she returns home, where she "took up the purple, sat down on her seat,[7] and drew out the thread." The angel returns at this very moment with his announcement, and this is what we see in the icon. It is an important detail that Mary is engaged in the work of weaving a new *veil of the Temple*. As Margaret Barker has explained (at least to my satisfaction), the veil of the Temple symbolized the visible creation.[8] Beyond it was the representation of the unseen abode of God (the Holy of Holies). In the icon, then, the thread for weaving the veil that we see in Mary's hands signifies the materiality assumed by Christ: his "flesh," as Hebrews 10:19–20 puts it straightforwardly: "Therefore, brothers, having the confidence to enter into the Holy of Holies by the blood of Jesus—by a way fresh and living, which he opened for us through the veil, which is to say, through his flesh."[9] And, of course, we should not forget the rending of the Temple veil when Christ dies (Mark 15:38 and parallels).[10] The thread in Mary's hand points to the incarnation and the cross simultaneously.

Finally, the icon of the Annunciation also reflects back to us an image of ourselves, in whom Christ is "born." This idea, far older than that of the

7. As Margaret Barker mentions in a footnote (*Christmas*, 155), the word for "seat" here is *thronos*, "which can be a throne, or a special chair of office"—and it is, in fact, a "throne" that we see in the icon.

8. See Barker, *Temple Mysticism*, 44.

9. D. B. Hart, *The New Testament*, 447.

10. In John's Gospel, in which Jesus reveals himself as the true Temple of God (John 2:19–21), the rending of the Temple's veil in the Synoptic Gospels is virtually paralleled by the rending of his flesh by the soldier's lance: "But one of the soldiers pierced his side with a spear, and at once there came out blood and water" (John 19:34). The implication may be that this was in fulfillment of prophecies that foretold that out of the Temple and Jerusalem would flow renewing waters (cf. Ezek 47:1-12; Zech 14:8; Joel 3:18; see also Rev 22:1–2).

"imitation of Christ," is a way of saying that we are united to Christ, that he "abides in us" as we "abide in him" (John 15:4). It also indicates that he "grows" within us, and that over time we more and more come to share his mind and live accordingly. The growth is gradual (cf. Mark. 4:26–29).

"*The Holy Spirit*, it was said, *shall come upon thee, and the power of the Most High shall overshadow thee*," wrote Origen (c. 184–c. 253). "The birth of Christ took its inception from the shadow; yet not in Mary only did his nativity begin with overshadowing; in you, too, if you are worthy, the Word of God is born" (*2nd Homily on the Song of Songs*).[11] Likewise, the words of Ambrose of Milan (c. 340–397): "A believing soul both conceives and brings forth the Word of God."[12] Dozens more could be cited. But, valuably for us, this nurturing notion of the "birth of Christ" within our selves became associated with contemplation and the work of silence, as patristic and medieval writers attest.

A fine later example of this can be seen in the writings of Johannes Tauler (c. 1300–1361). In a sermon on the Annunciation,[13] unsurprisingly, he suggests a procedure for those desiring to practice meditation. To grasp the points he makes in his homily, we must understand that he is referring specifically to the time we set aside for silent meditation. Tauler writes: "He, therefore, who desires to commune more and more with himself; and to find himself in the Source, in God, and to be conscious of God in his heart . . . must copy the likeness and the bright mirror of our Lady."

He then tells us what he means by "copying" Mary: "First, [the one seeking to meditate in silence] must turn away from all transitory things, and gather up the powers of his mind, and commune with himself, and pass over out of self into God, Who is present within him, in the innermost parts of his spirit . . . that there he may be united with and become one spirit with God; and there God will work in him." Practitioners of Zen—so similar in its basics to classical Christian contemplative practice—as well as of other forms of meditation might say that concentration on the breath, allowing our thoughts to come and go, but not "following after" them, is one helpful way to begin "turning from transitory things" and "communing with oneself." Tauler continues: "Thus we must remain empty, bare and dead

11. Origen, *The Song of Songs*, 293.

12. Ambrose of Milan, *Commentary on Luke*. Quotation from Wright, *Readings for the Daily Office*, 469.

13. Tauler, *The Inner Way*, 80–82. I ask readers to forgive the exclusive use of masculine pronouns in the excerpts, but I am quoting from an early twentieth-century rendering of a fourteenth-century text.

to all around us . . . Then man will be lifted up in himself by God above all powers into the wilderness of the Godhead . . . so that the Divine Birth will take place without let or hindrance in our spirits, in our souls, and also spiritually in our bodies."

It should be remembered that Tauler preached this in a *sermon*. In other words, he had no hesitancy about teaching contemplative practice from the pulpit. To meditate and do the work of silence, Tauler might say, one need only begin and stick with it. It is less difficult than one might suppose. Mary had only to say, "Be it done to me according to your word" for Christ to be conceived in her. Nothing else was necessary. And that mere act of receptivity may well be understood as the pure essence of prayer. Sometimes dry, sometimes dull, sometimes beset by distractions inner and outer, still—with perseverance—the contemplative work of silence can bear fruit in us as well.

The Second Mystery

The Visitation of Mary to Elizabeth

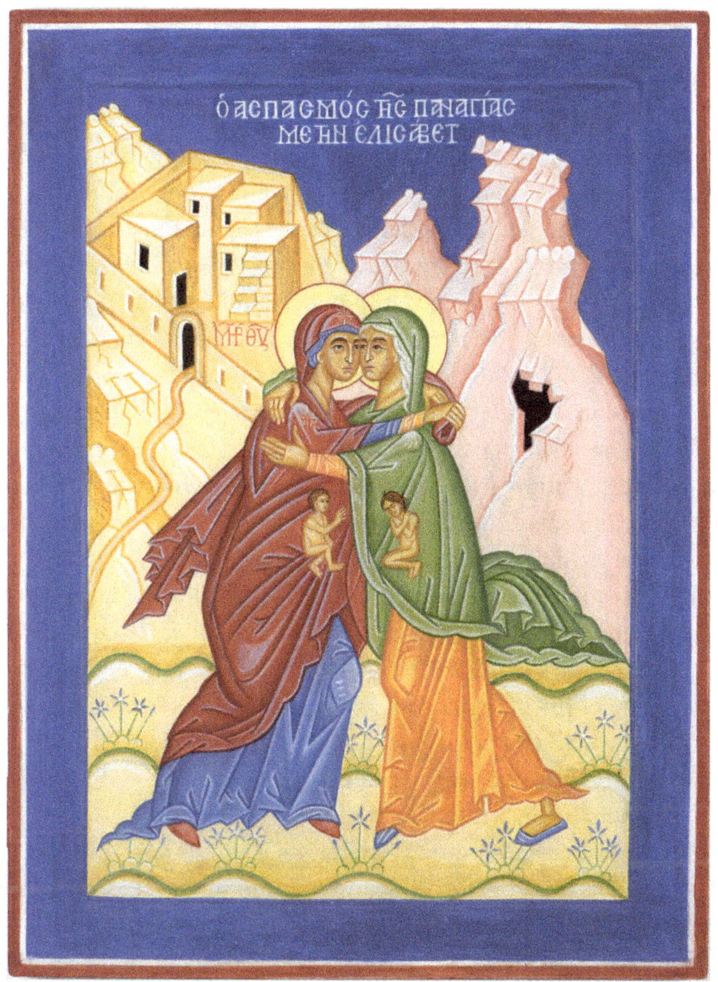

Readings for reflection:

Luke 1:36–56; *The Protevangelium of James*, Chapter 12

A note of joy rings throughout the story of the Visitation of Mary to Elizabeth, the mother of John the Baptist. Ain Karin is the traditional site of their meeting, a town set in a valley in the hill country west of Jerusalem. When Mary greets her, Elizabeth is immediately "filled with the Holy Spirit" and exclaims loudly, "Blessed are you among women, and blessed is the fruit of your womb! And why is this granted me, that the mother of my Lord should come to me? For behold, when the voice of your greeting came to my ears, the babe in my womb leaped for joy" (Luke 1:41–44). As we have noted more than once, "behold" is an important word. When we see or hear it, we are meant to pause and ponder.

The scene is that of two women greeting one another—two mothers bearing in their wombs two wonderful conceptions. But the picture is deeper than it looks, as the icon shows. It reveals something about their unborn children, a foreshadowing that these two lives would be intertwined in the coming years. We are given to understand that in the heart of one of these babes there is joy at the sound of Mary's voice. We might assume here that the unborn infant John is responding to the presence of the Lord within Mary, but a careful reading suggests that he is responding to "the voice" of "the mother of my Lord." Indeed, the *Protevangelium* strengthens the latter interpretation. In that version of the story, Elizabeth says to Mary: "The child within me leaped and blessed *you*" (*Prot.*, 12; emphasis mine). To which Mary replies, looking up to heaven: "Who am I, Lord, that all the generations of the earth are blessing me?" This question of Mary's is echoed in Luke, where we see that Mary's "song"—the *Magnificat*—makes a declaration similar to her words in the *Protevangelium*: "[F]or he has regarded the low estate of his handmaiden. For behold, henceforth all generations will call me blessed" (Luke 1:48; note, again, the word "behold"—*idou*). The importance—both in the sense of rank and significance—of Mary in this story should not be underestimated.

To see this, we need only consider what the phrase "Mother of the Lord" implies in this context. The term referred to the "queen mother" in the times of Judah's and Israel's kings, and this is undoubtedly the intended association here. The mother of the king held high status in the kingdom.[14] One cannot understand the court intrigue of 1 Kings 1, for example, and Nathan the prophet's soliciting of Bathsheba to involve herself in it on behalf of her son, Solomon, without some idea of what was at stake for her if she should fail to influence David to name her son as his royal successor (see 1 Kgs 1:11–31). Her own future preeminent position at court could

14. The mothers of the kings in Jerusalem are listed with the names of their sons in the books of the Kings: 1 Kgs 14:21; 15:2, 10; 2 Kgs 12:1; 14:2; 15:2, 33; 18:2; 21:1, 19; 22:1; 23:31, 36. Cf., too, 1 Kgs 15:13.

only be assured with Solomon's accession. Reading between the lines, it seems reasonable to assume that Nathan was counting on her ambitions both for her son and for herself. If Solomon took the throne, she would become the "Mother of the Lord" in the kingdom.

To refer, then, as Elizabeth does here to Mary as "Mother of the Lord" is to suggest quite a lot. Both the Gospel of Luke and the *Protevangelium*, which also uses the phrase, reflect the early Christian affirmation of Jesus' Messiahship. More pointedly still, Mary is not merely called "the Mother of *the* Lord" by Elizabeth, but "the Mother of *my* Lord"—a term used for the enthroned king in Psalm 110:1 ("The LORD said to *my* Lord: Sit at my right hand"), and regarded in later times as a title of the coming Davidic Messiah. Within Elizabeth's declaration, then, is a confession of the church's faith: "Jesus is Lord" (cf. Matt 12:3–8; Rom 10:9; 1 Cor 12:3). We also see in this not only the seeds for the later veneration of Mary in the tradition, but, in fact, a measure of veneration already in evidence.[15]

Although there is some manuscript evidence to suggest that Luke 1:46 originally read "she said" rather than "Mary said" before the verses of the *Magnificat*, there is little doubt that the song (based on the song of Hannah in 1 Samuel 2) has been rightly ascribed to Mary and not Elizabeth in the text. As already noted, the words of Mary in the *Protevangelium* back up that assumption.

In the "song," Mary gives glory to God on her own behalf, in thanksgiving for what God has wrought in her. In other words, she praises God as an individual for the gift within her body. But that is not the whole of it. She also praises God, not just as an individual, but *as a corporate person*. Her "I" is also a *collective* "I," as the song makes clear: "He has shown strength with his arm," she says, "he has scattered the proud in the imagination of their hearts, he has put down the mighty from their thrones, and exalted those of low degree; he has filled the hungry with good things, and the rich he has sent empty away" (Luke 1:51–53). With these words, she shows herself to be in solidarity with her people—with "[God's] servant Israel"—and at one with the poor, the hungry, and the humble. She rejoices in the hope that the rich and powerful will be overthrown, justice for the oppressed will be revealed, and those in need will find comfort, fullness, and refuge. Jesus will say things just as radical and even more pointedly just a few short chapters later (see,

15. In addition to the clear reference to "queen mother" in Elizabeth's greeting, there is also possibly—though the notion is speculative—a veiled allusion to the Ark of the Covenant as a type of the pregnant Mary in Luke 1:56. Compare that verse, with its mention of "three months," with 2 Samuel 6:11 and 1 Chronicles 13:14.

for example, Luke 6:20–26, in which he blesses the poor and oppressed and pronounces maledictions on the wealthy and callous). Mary's "song" is thus not about Mary alone, but about the conditions of her people and the new conditions she desires to see. She stands in the place of the "Daughter of Zion" or Wisdom, perhaps, and implores God through her praises on behalf of her "children." She represents them all, her individuality fully integrated with the "corporate personhood" of her people.

If, in our last commentary, we emphasized the solitary and contemplative aspect of Christian spirituality, this mystery and the words of the *Magnificat* should put us in mind that we are—like Mary—microcosms of the whole. There is no genuine Christian spirituality that is isolated and oblivious of the social realities around us. Mary's prayer of praise reflects the situation of her own time and place. Our prayers likewise cannot be dissociated from the needs and realities of our social contexts.

Today, despite the life and teachings of Jesus, the world still groans under the weight of rich and powerful oppressors, of those more interested in increasing their own wealth and prestige than in assisting those who suffer denigration, hunger, and poverty. Corporations control governments and create conflicts; refugees, migrants, and immigrants meet with little or no welcome from wealthy nations, and often with hostility; the marginalized and poor can expect very little in the way of help, even from those professing to be followers of Christ, and their desperation is more often than not ignored by those materially better off than they—indeed, the poor are frequently resented just for being poor; the environment is exploited and poisoned for profit, and people suffer the consequences in loss of health and property. The list of intractable—and in numerous cases, unnecessary—injustices is exceedingly long.

If Mary's "song" means anything at all, it means that the Messiah enters into a world of unmet needs. It means that we ourselves are no more disconnected from those with pressing needs around us and around the globe right now than Mary was to her people in Galilee in her own day. We are all "corporate persons," not merely "individuals," when it comes down to it. How we respond in our prayers and action to that inescapable reality is essential to understanding what it means to follow Jesus.

The Third Mystery

The Nativity of Jesus

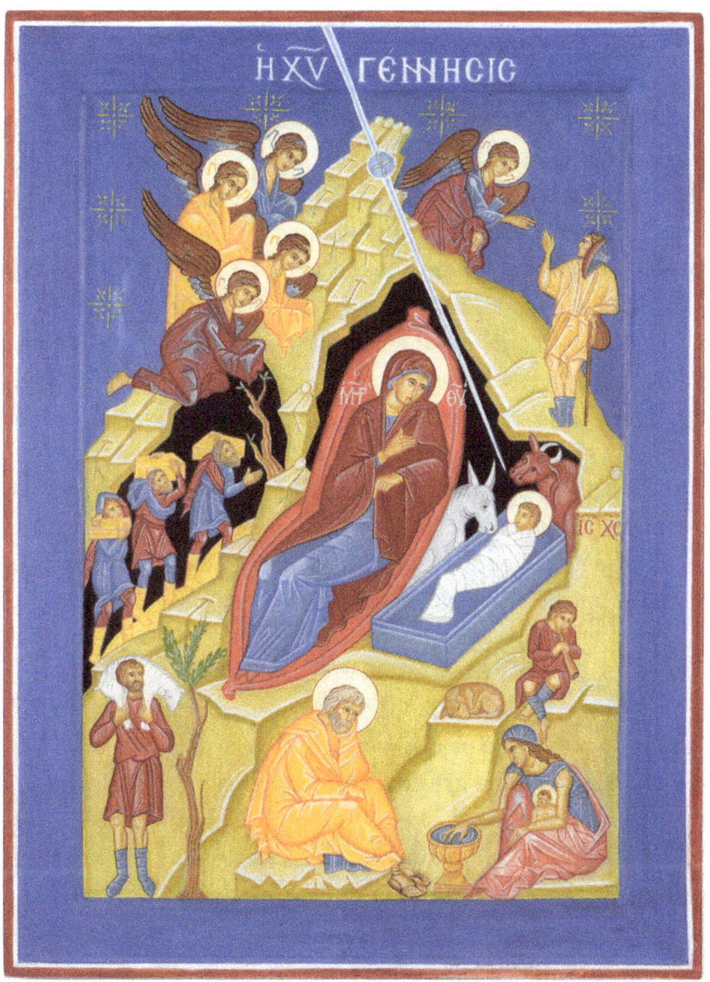

Readings for reflection:

> Luke 2:1–20; Matthew 1:18–2:12; *The Protovangelium of James*, Chapters 17–20

The Gospel of Luke does not say what sort of place it was where Jesus was born. We are told that he was laid in an animal's feeding trough, because Bethlehem was overcrowded on account of the census and there was no better place available. But feeding troughs could be found in houses. Animals were often kept indoors after dark on the ground floor. Luke could have meant that Jesus was born in a house where there was no vacant space left in the upper quarters or on the flat rooftop, which were customary places for sleeping. The tradition of Western Christmas art, ever since the time of Francis of Assisi, portrays him not in a crowded house, however, but in a wooden or stone stable, such as might have been seen throughout medieval Europe. But earlier Christian art and that of the East to this day, following the tradition found in the *Protevangelium*, depicts Christ's birth in a cave of the earth, as we see it in our icon.

The icon has a number of figures for us to note: the angels and the shepherds (Luke, *Protevangelium*), the magi traveling with their gifts (Matthew, *Protevangelium*), the midwife preparing to bathe the child (she is a character who appears in the *Protevangelium*), the ox and the ass worshipping the infant Christ,[16] a curled-up sleeping shepherd's dog (who has strayed into the scene), Joseph seated in apparent contemplation of the mysterious birth, and in the center of it all the Virgin Mother reclining before the cave's entrance. As for the cave, although it is not a "biblical" feature, it is certainly part of ancient tradition and evocative of what, in fact, are biblical associations. The cave, in fact, merits some special attention.

The first of these biblical associations, perhaps not one that is immediately obvious, is Genesis 2:7: "Then the LORD God formed man of dust from the ground." Irenaeus of Lyons, the second-century Syrian bishop whose see was in Gaul, makes the connection explicit: "While the earth was still *virgin*, God took dust and formed the man who was the beginning of humanity. Therefore, our Lord, recapitulating this man, used in a sense, the same means of taking on flesh when he was born of a *virgin*

16. The ox and ass are, of course, familiar characters in every crèche and manger scene. Their presence in the traditional tableau has sometimes been explained in rather ingenious ways, too elaborate to comment on here. But the most immediate explanation is the one we find reflected in *The Gospel of Pseudo-Matthew*, an eighth- or ninth-century apocryphal work: "On the third day after the birth of our Lord Jesus Christ holy Mary went out from the cave, and went into a stable and put her child in a manger, and an ox and an ass worshipped him. Then was fulfilled that which was said through the prophet Isaiah: '*The ox knows his owner and the ass his master's crib*' (Isa. 1:3). Thus the beasts, ox and ass, with him between them, unceasingly worshipped him. Then was fulfilled that which was said through the prophet Habakkuk: '*Between two beasts are you known*' (cf. Hab. 3:2, LXX)." Hennecke, *New Testament Apocrypha*, 410.

by the will and Wisdom of God" (emphasis mine).[17] "Earth" in Hebrew is *'adamah* (feminine), and from it is derived the name "Adam"—meaning "earthling." In the early church, the concept of the "virgin earth" giving birth to Adam was a common analogy to the virgin Mary giving birth to Christ (the "last Adam"; 1 Cor 15:45). We see it also, for instance, in *The Gospel of Philip*, an early Christian text later deemed to be "gnostic" (a loaded term that has itself become somewhat suspect among scholars): "Adam came from two virgins, the Spirit [the word "spirit" is feminine in gender] and the virgin earth. Christ was born of a virgin to correct the fall that occurred in the beginning."[18]

So, we have the analogy of two "virgins" in early Christianity: the earth and Mary. There is another, equally relevant biblical analogy that we find, for example, in Psalm 139—that between a mother's womb and the earth: "For thou didst form my inward parts, thou didst knit me together *in my mother's womb* . . . my frame was not hidden from thee, when I was being made in secret, intricately wrought *in the depths of the earth*" (Ps 139:13, 15; emphasis mine). This primitive association of the womb and the earth, by the way, helps to explain one original aspect of the custom of burial in the earth: it is a return to the "mother" of us all, "Mother Earth" (usually with the hope of some version of rebirth attached).[19] And, need we remind ourselves, that it is from a *cave* in the earth following his burial that Christ rose from the dead and became the author, in Christian belief, of our and all creation's rebirth? It is not too much to read in the traditional imagery of the church, as we see it exemplified in our icon here, a correlation between the Virgin Mother of Christ, the cave of his birth, and the cave of his resurrection. Among the aspects of this multivalent symbol of the cave as it appears in Christian iconography, then, we can clearly recognize an allusion to the sheer *earthiness* of the incarnation. The Son and Word assumes earthy materiality, and "materiality" means literally substance derived "from the mother"—the *mater*.

The birth of Christ is not only the uncreated and immaterial entering into the created and earthly, but also the timeless entering into time. This is illustrated in a moving passage from the *Protevangelium* (one not to be

17. Irenaios, *The Preaching of the Apostles*, (ch. 31), 47.

18. *The Gospel of Philip*, 71:16–21. Meyer, *The Nag Hammadi Scriptures*, 176.

19. Note the icon of the crucifixion of Christ in this book (the fifteenth mystery of the rosary), and the small "cave" depicted at the base of the cross, in which—as a symbol of our common death—the interred bones of Adam are visible.

found in every version of the book, incidentally), which apparently draws its inspiration from the passage in the book of Wisdom that reads: "For while gentle silence enveloped all things . . . thy all-powerful word leaped from heaven" (Wis 18:14–15). The story is told in the first person, as if by Joseph, and in it we have the moment of the descent of Christ causing all things to freeze their movements and linger in stillness for a span of time. (Again, we have to bear in mind that these narratival elements are mythopoeic in nature. Literal history is not the author's concern, *meaning* is. And religious meaning is best conveyed by imagery and metaphor, not systems or doctrinal formulas or dry theologizing.) This is, in fact, a noticeably contemplative moment in the book. It assumes the nature of a motionless tableau, the characters described in it reminding us of the figures depicted in the icon:

> Now I, Joseph, was walking, and (yet) I did not walk, and I looked up to the air and saw the air in amazement. And I looked up at the vault of heaven, and saw it standing still and the birds of the heaven motionless. And I looked at the earth, and saw a dish placed there and workmen lying round it, with their hands in the dish. But those who chewed did not chew, and those who lifted up anything lifted up nothing, and those who put something in their mouth put nothing (to their mouth), but all had their faces turned upwards. And behold, sheep were being driven and (yet) they did not come forward, but stood still; and the shepherd raised his hand to strike them with his staff, but his hand remained up. And I looked at the flow of the river, and saw the mouths of the kids over it and they did not drink. And then all at once everything went on its course (again). (*Prot.*, 18)[20]

When Joseph, accompanied by the midwife, returns to the cave after that strange event, they see a sight reminiscent of the glorious cloud that appeared to the Israelites in the wilderness, descended on the Temple of Solomon, and would later appear in the account of Christ's transfiguration (see, for example, Exod 24:15–18; 1 Kgs 8:10–11; Matt 17:5): "And [Joseph and the midwife] went to the place of the cave, and behold, a bright [other texts read "dark"] cloud overshadowed the cave" (*Prot.*, 18).[21]

For the practitioner of meditation, the cave's significance also has to do with one's "heart," in which God is "born." The "cave of the heart" is a

20. Hennecke, *New Testament Apocrypha*, 383–84.
21. Hennecke, *New Testament Apocrypha*, 383–84.

very ancient metaphor for the interior depths of a person. It appears, for example, in the *Upanishads* as the inner "place" where *brahman* is encountered (for example: "[T]he fire-altar that leads to heaven . . . lies hidden in the cave of the heart"; "[*Brahman*] is right here within those who see, hidden within the cave of their heart").[22] The monk's cell, often a cave, and the monk's heart are analogous in Christian desert spirituality. "Go, sit in your cell, and your cell will teach you everything," says Abba Moses the Black. The cave in the art of the Christian icon "is the heart, the monk's cell, the holy of holies all at once."[23] Whether by intention or by accident, then, the *Protevangelium*, with its picture of all things rendered silent and still as the Word-made-flesh is born within the cave, is also a picture of the fruitful work of silence within the heart. The icon points to the secret of Christian contemplation in its depiction of the Nativity.

It is there that "Christ is born" within us, as we saw in the words of Johannes Tauler in our commentary on the Annunciation. Everything, for the disciple of Christ, depends on that presence taking shape and growing within. The power of the image of the Nativity is that it expresses an inner truth, an interior birth that promises a gradual transformation of our selves—"from glory to glory" (2 Cor 3:18).

22. *Katha Upanishad*, 3,1; *Mundaka Upanishad*, 3,1,7. Cited from Olivelle, *Upanishads*, 238, 275.

23. Pageau, "The Cave in the Nativity Icon."

The Fourth Mystery

The Presentation of Jesus in the Temple

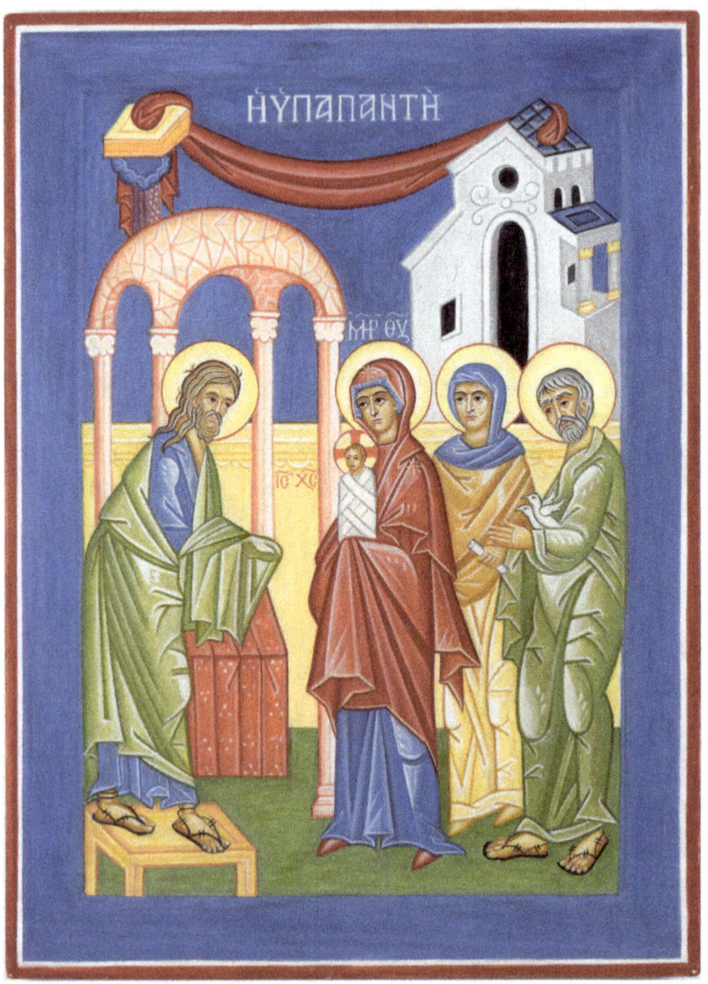

Reading for reflection:

Luke 2:22–40

The story of the Presentation in the Gospel of Luke never states outright that the "righteous and devout" Simeon was an old man. We are told that he was "looking for the consolation of Israel" and he is described as being the recipient of a divine revelation (Luke 2:25–26), but there is nothing explicitly said about his age. Still, there is strong implication that he was advanced in years. We are told that the other person who was present to witness the occasion, Anna the "prophetess," certainly was elderly ("she was of a great age, having lived with her husband seven years from her virginity, and as a widow till she was eighty-four"; Luke 2:36–37). But Simeon, for his part, speaks with the voice of one who is aged. We have the clue in the text where we are informed that "it had been revealed to him by the Holy Spirit that he should not taste death before he had seen the Lord's Christ" (Luke 2:26). And his "song" (known in the Latin West as the *Nunc dimittis*, where it has been chanted in the church's night prayers since ancient times) is one of faithful resignation to God and to death: "Lord, now lettest thou thy servant depart in peace, according to thy word" (Luke 2:29 KJV). Simeon and Anna in the Temple, it seems, represent the faithful older generation that is preparing to pass away. They are old and close to death, Luke seems to say, but they stand as witnesses of the new order that God is inaugurating.

The Gospel portrays this in spare and subtle fashion, as does our simple icon. The humility of Simeon and Anna is reflected in the plainness of the narrative: Simeon "took [Jesus] up in his arms and blessed God" (Luke 2:28); Anna "gave thanks to God, and spoke of [Christ] to all who were looking for the redemption of Jerusalem" (Luke 2:38). A modest but fervent faith is expressed here. God has promised, and the fulfillment of his promise is now manifested, and they rejoice. God is to be blessed and thanked for the light and glory they behold in the infant Jesus.

Readers of the narrative could perhaps take comfort in this scene of faith and thanksgiving, until they are abruptly jarred to renewed attention by the disturbing words Simeon speaks next to Mary directly. The old man becomes somber and prophesies that the light of this new dispensation will not shine without clouds of accompanying darkness—not even for the young mother standing before him. This young Messiah will prove to be "a sign spoken against" and he brings with him a piercing "sword." "This child is set for the fall and rising of many in Israel . . . and," Simeon says to Mary, "a sword will pierce through your own soul also" (Luke 2:34–35).

What possibly could be the meaning of "the sword" that will pierce even the soul of Mary as Luke's Gospel presents it? Often it is taken to be a reference to Mary's inner suffering as she saw her son put to death. But, while Mary as the *Mater Dolorosa* has had a long history in Christian devotion, and while it certainly has psychological potency for those whose piety tends to be more affective in nature, it is almost certainly not what is meant by Simeon's words in Luke. If we are to get at Luke's intended meaning, we must seek for it in that particular Gospel alone. There are two reasons for this. First, the Presentation account is only in Luke, and therefore its significance is peculiar to that particular book. And, second, the Gospel of Luke makes no mention of Mary being present at Jesus' crucifixion (that detail appears in the Gospel of John). The "sword," then, almost certainly must imply something other than Mary's inner suffering before her son's cross. We do, though, find three other instances in Luke that suggest a more consistent interpretation of Simeon's metaphor.

The first instance is the finding of Jesus in the Temple (our next mystery) and the sharp words that Jesus says to Mary and Joseph: "How is it that you sought me? Did you not know that I must be in my Father's house?" (Luke 2:49). Jesus says this after his mother, evidently pained by his disappearance, remonstrates with him: "Son, why have you treated us so?" Luke tells us that his parents "did not understand" Jesus' apparently unfeeling response to them, but that "his mother kept all these things in her heart" despite that (Luke 2:50–51). There is in Jesus' words something cutting, which certainly would have been taken by his parents to be a distancing of himself from them. We can, I think, see the piercing "sword" at work here.

The second instance occurs when Mary and Jesus' family members come to see him but are unable to reach him on account of the crowds. Instead of an unambiguous welcome by Jesus, however, they are again "distanced" by his words to them instead. His words are notably softer in tone in Luke's Gospel than how they are rendered in the parallel accounts in Matthew and Mark, but they are stinging nonetheless: "My mother and my brothers are those who hear the word of God and do it" (Luke 8:19–21; compare Matt 12:46–50; Mark 3:31–35). Here, too, we very likely see Simeon's "sword" in action.

And later still we read of another incident, found only in Luke, in which a woman in the crowd around Jesus cries out, "Blessed is the womb that bore you, and the breasts that you sucked!" Jesus replies to her with seeming curtness, but in words similar to his response to his mother and brothers' visit in chapter 8: "Blessed rather are those who hear the word of God and keep it!" (Luke 11:27–28). If it were not the case that Luke's readers would already know from the Gospel's earliest chapters that Mary had demonstrated her willing obedience to God and faithfully kept his word in her heart, this declaration of Jesus could seem to us to be unbearably dismissive and withering. Early readers of Luke's Gospel would also quite probably have detected in this passage the sharp "sword" of Simeon's prophecy.

The "sword" as metaphor for "the word of God" seems to be the best interpretation of the image, if we understand that much abused term ("word of God") is not a reference to "Scripture." In the early church "the word of God" signified something more existential and direct in nature, something far greater in scope than those written texts early believers held to be sacred. In fact, as it is used by Jesus in the Gospels, it means above all else his own message about the kingdom and what being his disciple entails. As we saw in both 8:19–21 and 11:27–28 above, "hearing the word of God and doing/keeping it" was the focus of Jesus' challenging words in both instances. As he says elsewhere, his teaching is a "sword" that could bring division even within formerly cohesive families: "Do you think that I have come to give peace on earth? No, I tell you, but rather division; for henceforth in one house there will be [division]" (Luke 12:51–52). His call to follow him was urgent and critical: "If any one comes to me and does not hate his own father and mother and wife and children and brothers and sisters, yea, and even his own life, he cannot be my disciple" (Luke 14:26). These are harrowing words to our ears, and rightly so, but our ears belong to a very different culture than that of Jesus. His demand is to be understood culturally as typical rabbinical hyperbole—an overstatement to stress the urgency of his plea. Nonetheless, here is Simeon's "sword" on full display.

The image of a sword for the word of God, of course, is found elsewhere in the New Testament. We see it in Ephesians 6:17 and Revelation 19:13–15; but it is Hebrews 4:12 that may come closest to the imagery of the "sword" that "will pierce through [Mary's] own soul": "For the word of God is living and active, sharper than any two-edged sword, piercing to the division of soul and spirit, of joints and marrow, and discerning the thoughts and intentions of the heart." The overall message, then, is pointed like a sword: Jesus' call to discipleship means "hearing" him and "doing" what he instructs, regardless of one's status or position or even one's flesh-and-blood relationship to him. As we hear him say about another Mary in the same Gospel, "Mary has chosen the good portion [by sitting and listening to Jesus' words], which shall not be taken away from her" (Luke 10:42).

And here, lastly, we are reminded again of the Virgin Mary's symbolic role. She is, as we have already seen, an image for us of wisdom, the church, and each Christian soul precisely because she heard the word of God and guarded it in her heart. She is the model disciple, as many commentators have noted. She reminds us that, at the core of our practice, is an ongoing attentiveness to Jesus' teachings, allowing them to take deep root in us: "The seed [the sower sows] is the word of God" (Luke 8:11). He is the sower and his scattered words are to be our daily meditation and guide our action in the world. As it was for Mary, his word will also be for us a "sword" at times, convicting us deeply, challenging us to change, and piercing our own souls also—and that for our own good.

The Fifth Mystery

The Finding of Jesus in the Temple at Age Twelve

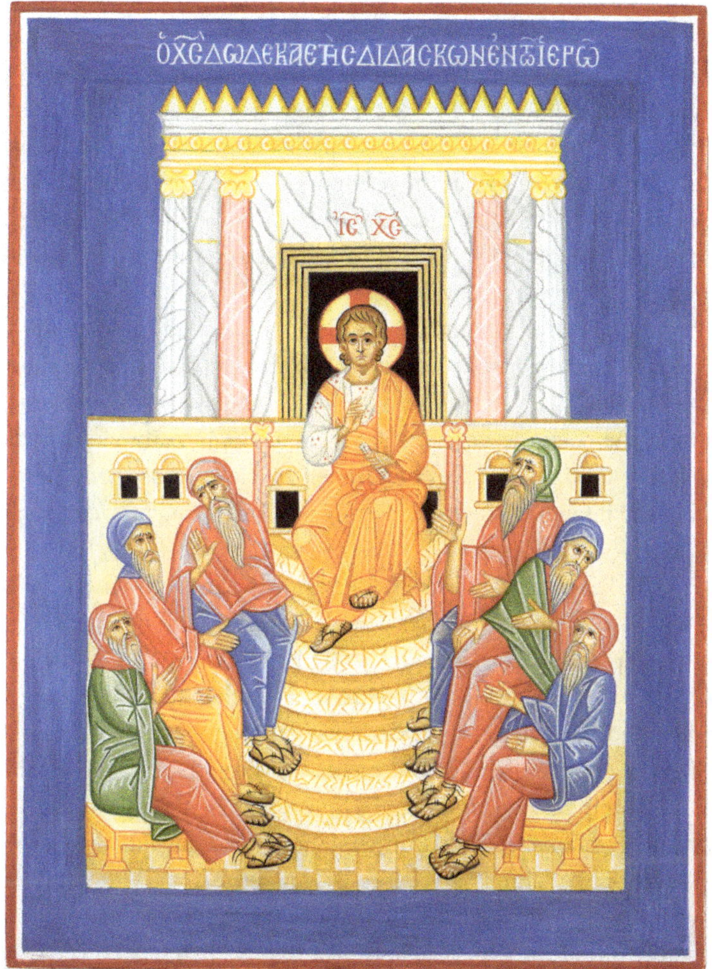

Reading for reflection:

Luke 2: 41–52

On one level, the story of the finding of the twelve-year-old Jesus in the Temple by his searching parents follows a common pattern in ancient historical literature. As *The Jewish Annotated New Testament* notes, "Stories of heroes' prodigious wisdom are conventional." The same annotation goes on to provide a short list of examples from ancient writers, concluding with the first-century Jewish historian Josephus, who wrote with little regard for modesty: "[W]hen I was a child of fourteen years of age . . . the high priests and principal men of the city [Jerusalem] frequently came to me together, to know my opinion about the accurate understanding of points of the law" (*Life*, 9).[24] And, as if to underscore the conventional nature of the story, the Gospel of Luke, which has echoed already Hannah's "song" of 1 Samuel 2:1–10 with Mary's "song" in the Visitation, here has verse 52 ("And Jesus increased in wisdom and stature, and in favor with God and man") echo 1 Samuel 2:26: "Now the boy Samuel continued to grow both in stature and in favor with the LORD and with men."

On another level, though, Luke is looking ahead to what will come later in the ministry of Jesus by foreshadowing in this account about the boy the teaching style of the adult. Already evident in the preternatural wisdom of the young Jesus, Luke is saying, is the fully developed wisdom of the future teacher. This can be gleaned by closely observing how Luke describes the interchange of questioning and answering between Jesus and "the teachers" in the Temple.

First, Luke tells us that Jesus is found "sitting among"—literally, "in the midst of"—the teachers. In other words, they surround him as the crowds and his disciples will also do later during his discourses. The very posture of sitting, in fact, was itself the posture of a teacher. Second, we are given to understand that when Jesus *questions* his interlocutors' teachings ("[he was] listening to them and asking them questions"), they presumably respond with their *answers*, and then he *answers* them in return ("and all who heard him were amazed at his understanding and his *answers*"). We can presume that Luke is implying that Jesus' answers carry with them a finality and authority that astounds the teachers. As Origen noted, "He Himself answers the questions which he had asked . . . Sometimes Jesus questions, sometimes He replies, as we said above: and truly astonishing are His questions, yet more wondrous are His replies."[25] As a reader of the Gospels can easily recognize, this is the adult style of the teacher Jesus. A particularly trenchant example of this back-and-forth question-and-answer style occurs while he is teaching in the Temple towards the end of his ministry, in

24. Levine and Brettler, *The Jewish Annotated New Testament*, 103.

25. Quoted in Toal, *The Sunday Sermons of the Great Fathers*, 242–43.

less irenic circumstances than here. There he is confronted by "the chief priests and the scribes with the elders":

> [They] said to him, "Tell us by what authority you do these things, or who it is who gave you this authority." He answered them, "I also will ask you a question; now tell me, Was the baptism of John from heaven or from men?" And they discussed it with one another, saying, "If we say, 'From heaven,' he will say, 'Why did you not believe him?' But if we say, 'From men,' all the people will stone us; for they are convinced that John was a prophet." So they answered that they did not know whence it was. And Jesus said to them, "Neither will I tell you by what authority I do these things." (Luke 20:1–8)

This high view of Jesus as the teacher who brings wisdom with him into the Temple, even while still a boy among the elders, is beautifully presented in our icon. Behind him we see the grand entrance to the Holy of Holies, reminding us perhaps of the mouth of the cave in the Nativity icon. Solrunn has been careful here to render the imposing structure in her icon as a stylized, simplified version of the historical Temple of Herod the Great. On either side of Jesus, along the steps, sit the teachers of Israel. He is seated in their midst in the place of authority, the Lord suddenly come to his Temple (cf. Mal 3:1). In his left hand he holds a scroll, another symbol of his divine authority. In the narrative, when his worried parents find him and ask him, "Son, why have you treated us so?," his answer is: "Did you not know that I must be in my Father's house?" (Luke 2:48, 49)—also indicative of his authority and mission. He comes now to the Temple as the teacher; later, he will return as the judge (Luke 19:45–46). However, so that everything is done properly, at its appointed time, we are told that "he went down with [his parents] and came to Nazareth, and was obedient to them; and his mother kept all these things in her heart" (Luke 2:51). His divine authority is subsumed and expressed by his willing humility.

Before concluding here, I return to an incarnational theme we have highlighted more than once already in this first set of mysteries. The great German mystic Meister Eckhart (c. 1260–c. 1328)[26] makes the connection for us between the example of the wise mother of Jesus, who kept these things in her heart, and that "birth" of Christ's presence within the

26. Eckhart was the teacher of Johannes Tauler, whom we cited in the first and third mysteries above.

contemplative soul's core. "We read in the gospel," he wrote, "that when our Lord was twelve years old he went to the temple at Jerusalem."

> [Mary and Joseph] looked for him in the crowds and still they could not find him. Furthermore, they had lost him among the [Temple] crowds and had to go back where they came from. When they got back to their starting point, they found him.

From this, Eckhart draws out a truth for us in our daily practice of silent meditative prayer:

> Thus it is true that, if you are to experience this noble birth, you must depart from all crowds and go back to the starting point, the core [of the soul] out of which you came. The crowds are the agents of the soul and their activities: memory, understanding, and will, in all their diversifications. You must leave them all: sense perception, imagination, and all that you discover in self or intend to do. After that, you may experience that birth—but otherwise not—believe me! . . .
>
> This work [birth], when it is perfect, will be due solely to God's action while you have been passive. If you really forsake your own knowledge and will, then surely and gladly God will enter with his knowledge shining clearly.[27]

Mary and Joseph are exemplars for us. They return to their "starting point," which is the Temple. The Temple, in this analogy, becomes a symbol for our own "core" or "heart"—our starting point, "out of which [we] came." Like Mary and Joseph in their search, we eschew the "crowds." In Eckhart's treatment, the "crowds" are, to simplify his meaning, our many crowded thoughts. In the silence of our hearts, then, which comes with regular practice, we are to become temples in which Christ abides and teaches us without words. This is the inner "birth" of Christ in us, the extension of his incarnation.

27. Blakney, *Meister Eckhart*, 118–19.

Second Set: The "Luminous" Mysteries

Revelation

The Sixth Mystery

The Baptism of Jesus

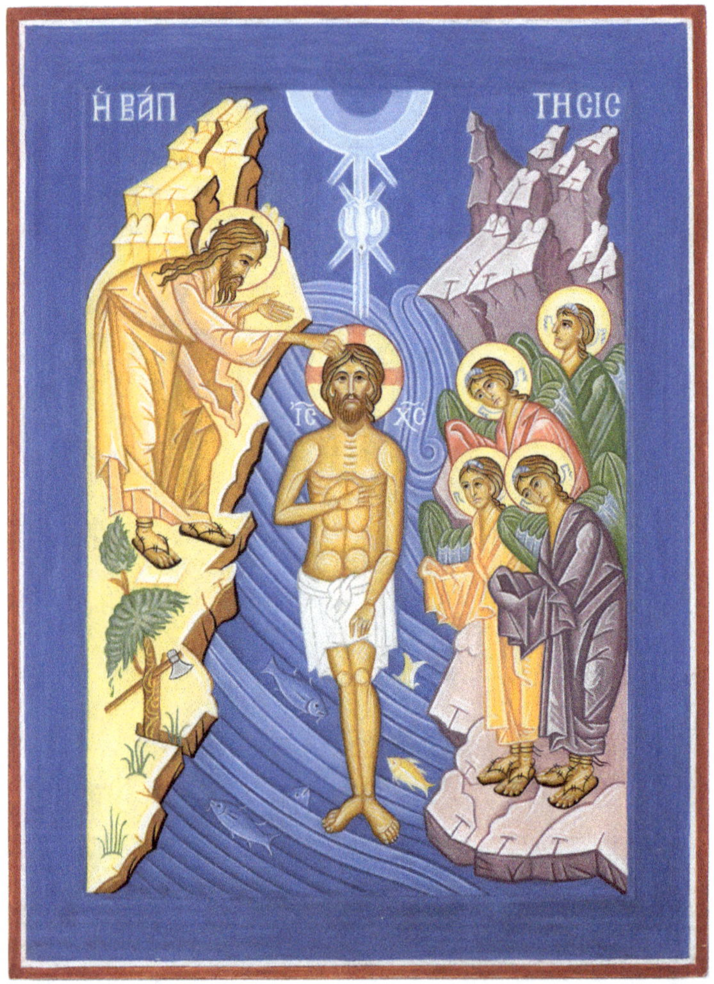

Readings for reflection:

Mark 1:1–11; Matthew 3:1–17; Luke 3:1–22; John 1:29–34

How did the early church make sense of the somewhat awkward fact that Jesus had been baptized by John the Baptist? Followers of Jesus the Messiah did not regard his "forerunner," after all, as Jesus' equal.

Although there is no account of Jesus in the role of John's disciple, it seems more likely than not that some such apprenticeship existed between them—a prospect which is not likely to scandalize most Christians today. But, for early Christians, given their high view of Jesus' status, there were questions that needed to be addressed about the relationship of Jesus to John, particularly as followers of the latter were still to be found—followers who did not see in Jesus John's successor or his superiority to him (in fact, veneration of John the Baptist continues to this day among the Mandaeans of Iran and Iraq and in diaspora communities in the West). The two most pressing questions for Christians were these: How was it that the greater had submitted to the cleansing rite administered by the lesser? And, how could it be that Jesus, understood as being without sin, had allowed himself to be baptized for the remission of sins?

One can see how these questions were treated in the earliest decades when we compare the four Gospel accounts. Mark's is the earliest, and there the baptism of Jesus is treated straightforwardly, with little elaboration. There is, of course, attention paid to Jesus' higher status. John clearly says that he is the forerunner of "he who is mightier than I, the thong of whose sandals I am not worthy to stoop down and untie" (Mark 1:7). In other words, the lesser acknowledges the greater. In Mark's Gospel, too, it is Jesus—not John—who sees "the heaven opened and the Spirit descending upon him like a dove" (Mark 1:10).

Matthew's account goes a step further than Mark's, making it unmistakably evident to his readers that Jesus is not baptized for the cleansing of sins. In a dialogue between Jesus and the Baptist, John seeks to prevent Jesus from being baptized by him: "I need to be baptized by you, and do you come to me?" Jesus reassures the hesitant John, telling him, "Let it be so now; for thus it is fitting for us to fulfill all righteousness"—a somewhat enigmatic reply, but one intended to bypass entirely the problem of a sinless Jesus receiving sinners' baptism (Matt 3:14–15). And in Matthew, as in Mark, the descent of the Spirit like a dove is Jesus' own, apparently private revelation.

Luke takes another tack. His description of Jesus' baptism is truncated to the point that we are only told what occurred after the event, while Jesus "was praying." As Jesus prays, "the heaven was [really, not figuratively] opened, and the Holy Spirit descended upon him *in bodily form, as a dove.*" In other words, Luke presents the Spirit's descent not merely as a subjective revelation to Jesus. In fact, the Spirit appears to be, in some sense, *incarnated* as a dove (Luke 3:21–22). (Luke tends elsewhere to emphasize physicality in a way that, say, Paul does not—for example, compare how Luke describes the resurrection body in 24:39 with how Paul understands it in 1 Corinthians 15:50.)

John, the last of the Gospels to be written, goes the furthest of all to avoid the problems inherent in Jesus' baptism. He omits it altogether. Jesus is never actually said to have been baptized in the fourth Gospel, not that it is denied either. It simply is not mentioned, and one can only surmise that the Gospel is probably not rejecting the event. Instead, John is said to baptize with water, but only as a preparation for Christ's coming—"that he might be revealed to Israel" (John 1:31). John even seems to be cognizant of Jesus' pre-incarnate existence: "After me comes a man who ranks before me, for he was before me" (John 1:30). And it is John, not Jesus, who sees the Spirit descend on Jesus as a sign and testimony. John declares: "I saw the Spirit descend as a dove from heaven, and it remained on him . . . [H]e who sent me to baptize with water said to me, 'He on whom you see the Spirit descend and remain, this is he who baptizes with the Holy Spirit" (John 1:32–33). So, again, we see the lesser witnessing to the greater. And there can be no doubt that this pre-existent incarnate man is sinless; the Baptist implies his blamelessness, in fact, when he introduces Jesus as "the Lamb of God, who takes away the sin of the world" (John 1:29; see v. 36).

It is, perhaps, John's Gospel—despite the fact that there is no direct mention of Jesus' baptism in it—that most influenced the development in later writers' interpretation of the event. Once it was allowed that in the person of Jesus the Logos of God, the author of creation, had entered the baptismal waters, the meaning of the event was permanently transfigured and took on a truly cosmic significance.

Our icon reflects this development. Picking up on the Christology of the "church fathers," Jesus' baptism is depicted here as a "theophany"—a manifestation or revelation of God acting in the world. As described in the Gospels, the heaven is opened above Jesus' head, and from it issues the voice of the invisible Father declaring him to be his Son (echoing the "kingly" Psalm 2:7), and the Holy Spirit in the form of a dove descends upon him. On the bank of the river waiting to attend Jesus are four angels, signifying his divine lordship. There are no crowds of people coming to be cleansed of their sins in the picture. Rather, what we behold in this depiction is not a "cleansing" of any person at all. Indeed, we have something quite nearly the reverse: it is a cleansing of the waters and, flowing from them, a cleansing of the world. In other words, the early church saw in Christ's baptism a revelation that God is a Trinity of Father, Son, and Spirit—God transcendent, God incarnate, and God indwelling—God encompassing all things, God with us (Emmanuel), God within us—and that this triune God was dynamically at work in creation to cleanse it and glorify it.

This is beautifully expressed for us by Gregory Nazianzus (c. 329–390) in his thirty-ninth *Oration*. Gregory sees in Jesus' baptism an encapsulation of his mission, his death and resurrection. More than that, he sees all those who are baptized into the body of Christ and also the entire creation joined to Christ and receiving a baptismal cleansing through him (he "takes away the sin of the world"). This is a poetic and spiritual interpretation, one that rewards meditation. "Christ is baptized," writes Gregory, "let us also go down with him, and rise with him . . . He comes to sanctify the Jordan for our sake and in readiness for us; he who is spirit and flesh comes to begin a new creation through the Spirit and water."

Jesus enters into the depths of the world, which God loves (John 3:16–17). Although, historically, there have been world-denying elements within Christianity, its essential message is nevertheless world-embracing. The Word becomes flesh and is one with all creation. Gregory can therefore write these words, with which I will conclude the commentary on this mystery:

> Jesus rises from the waters; the world rises with him. The heavens like Paradise with its flaming sword, closed by Adam for himself and his descendants, are rent open. The Spirit comes to him as to an equal, bearing witness to his Godhead. A voice bears witness to him from heaven, his place of origin . . .
>
> Be cleansed entirely and continue to be cleansed . . . [God] wants you to become a living force for humanity, lights shining in the world. You are to be radiant lights as you stand beside Christ, the great light, bathed in the glory of him who is the light of heaven.[1]

1. Wright, *Readings for the Daily Office*, 47–48.

The Seventh Mystery

The Wedding Feast at Cana

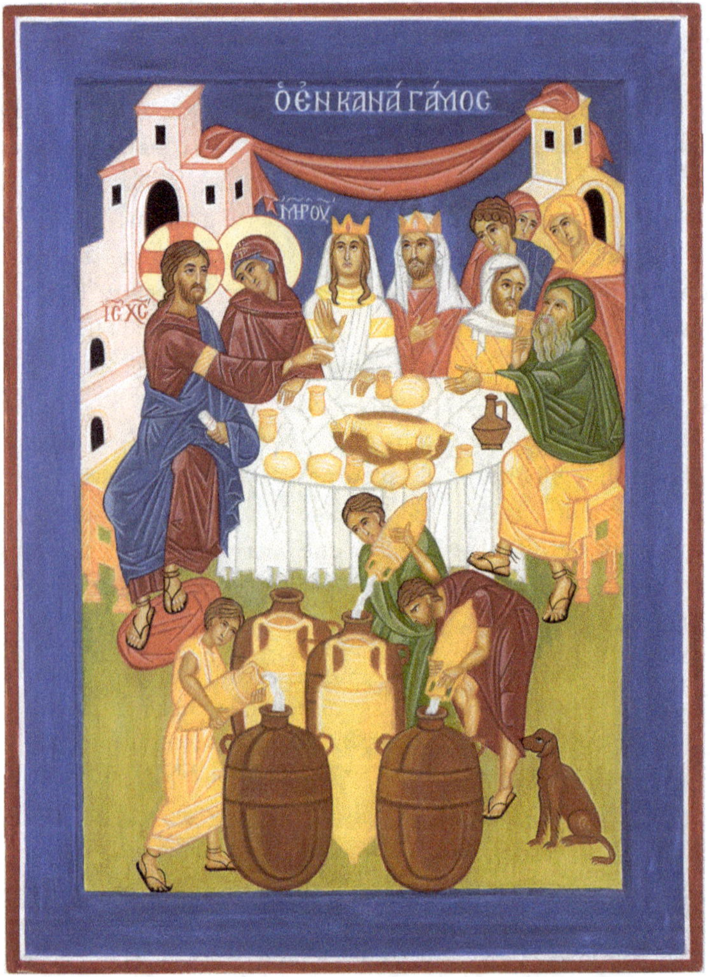

Reading for reflection:

John 2:1–12

One of the most striking features of the Gospel of John is its view of eschatology. "Eschatology" refers to "the end" (*eschaton*) of this present age and the transition to "the age to come." John's view of it is something like this: Because God the Logos has taken on flesh in Christ and rescued us from "perishing" (John 3:16), then the "end"—not in the sense of "finality," but in the sense of achieving the "goal"—has already been accomplished (see John 19:30). The incarnation has definitively revealed God to human beings. To encounter Jesus is also to "see" the invisible Father (John 14:9), because he and the Father are eternally "one," sharing the same divine nature (John 10:30; 1:1). What Christ finished on the cross, which with the resurrection constituted his "glorification" (John 12:23; 13:31–32; 17:1, 4–5), was the "tak[ing] away [of] the sin of the world" (John 1:29). By doing this, he carried out "the judgment of the world" and overthrew the power of its "ruler," the devil (John 12:31). John affirms that there is coming a "last day," but both the salvation and judgment of the cosmos have already, in effect, happened; all that is left for the future as the decisive criterion for each person's life is hearing and doing Jesus' sayings (John 12:47–50; see 5:24).

One of the many scriptural images for the *eschaton* is what is often called the "Messianic banquet" (Matt 8:11; Luke 22:30), a Semitic metaphor for celebration and abundance older than Christianity.[2] In the Gospels, the two feedings of the multitudes prefigure it and the Eucharist is a sacramental foreshadowing of it.[3] In the book of Revelation, picking up on the ancient Hebrew prophetic language about the union between Yahweh and his people as a marriage between a bride and her husband,[4] the eschatological image of joyful feasting is depicted as a marriage banquet: "Let us rejoice and exult and give him glory, for the marriage of the Lamb has come, and

2. In the Old Testament, the seeds for this eschatological concept can be found in such texts as Isaiah 25:6–8 and 55:1–2. In intertestamental literature, one can find it in various apocalyptic writings, e.g., 1 Enoch 62:14 ("The Lord of the Spirits will abide over them; they shall eat and rest and rise with that Son of Man forever and ever") and 2 Baruch 29:5–8 ("The earth will also yield fruits ten thousandfold. And on one vine will be a thousand branches, and one branch will produce a thousand clusters, and one cluster will produce a thousand grapes, and one grape will produce a cor of wine. And those who are hungry will enjoy themselves and they will, moreover, see marvels every day . . . And it will happen at that time that the treasury of manna will come down again from on high, and they will eat of it in those years because these are those who will have arrived at the consummation of time"). See Charlesworth, *The Old Testament Pseudepigrapha, Volume 1*, 44 and 630–31.)

3. The feeding of the five thousand appears in all four Gospels: Mark 6:30–44; Matt 14:13–21; Luke 9:10–17; John 6:1–13. The additional feeding of the four thousand appears only in Mark 8:1–10 and Matthew 15:32–39. For the Eucharist as prefiguring the Messianic banquet, see Mark 14:25; Matt 26:29; Luke 22:15–16, 18; 1 Cor 11:26.

4. Cf. Isa 54:5; 62:4–5; Jer 2:1–3; 3:20; Ezek 16:8; Hos 2:14–20.

his Bride has made herself ready . . . Blessed are those who are invited to the marriage supper of the Lamb" (Rev 19:7, 9).

The images of feasting and marriage as metaphors of salvation show up as early as the second chapter of the Gospel of Mark, the earliest of the canonical Gospels, bearing the metaphorical weight of eschatological expectation with them. When Jesus is questioned about his disciples' seemingly cavalier disregard for Jewish fasting customs ("Why do John's disciples and the disciples of the Pharisees fast, but your disciples do not fast?"), his answer is: "Can the wedding guests fast while the Bridegroom is with them? As long as they have the Bridegroom with them, they cannot fast. The days will come, when the Bridegroom is taken away from them, and then they will fast in that day." With that saying, he puts himself in the place of the eschatological bridegroom, presumably as a claim of Messianic status. If this assertion were not enough already to stir up his hearers, he caps it off with two parables calculated to unsettle them even more, one of which involves the symbol of wine: "No one sews a piece of unshrunk cloth on an old garment; if he does, the patch tears away from it, the new from the old, and a worse tear is made. And no one puts new wine into old wineskins; if he does, the wine will burst the skins, and the wine is lost, and so are the skins; but new wine is for fresh skins" (Mark 2:18–22; see Matt 9:14–17; Luke 5:33–39). In other words, with Jesus something *new in quality* has come on the scene and the old forms will not be sufficient to contain it. A transformation must occur.

Turning to the Gospel of John and our seventh mystery, Jesus changing water into wine—the first of his "signs," as John refers to Jesus' miracles—is performed at a marriage banquet and it corresponds to the scene above taken from Mark. There seems to be a direct echo between the two passages, in fact. As with the account in Mark, the Cana story appears early in John's narrative, in the second chapter. One aspect of John's Gospel that is essential to bear in mind when reading any passage from it is that it was understood by the early church to be a "spiritual" Gospel. By using that term *spiritual*, what was meant was that everything in it has "spiritual" significance, and to read it merely as a "literal" account is to handle it wrongly (to a lesser extent, the same must be said about the other Gospels, as well). So, for example, we should not overlook that—without explanation—the miraculous event is said to take place "on the third day" (John 2:1), possibly as a symbolic allusion to the resurrection, and possibly, too, as an allusion to God gathering the waters into seas on the third day of creation

(Gen 1:9–13). Similarly, as we said above, what Jesus performs throughout John's Gospel are "signs," not "miracles." They are, in other words, intended to indicate something beyond themselves—in this case, his identity and purpose. In the event of the sign performed at Cana, the transformation of water into wine was done in order to "manifest his glory," so that his disciples might "believe in him" (John 2:11). The story thus serves as a parable in John, and it makes a similar point as the one made in the account in Mark cited above, which is this: *something new has come into the world and the old order must change as a result.* Underscoring that interpretation, the remainder of John 2 is about the cleansing of the Temple by Christ (which, in a major departure from the Synoptic accounts, is placed early, not late, in Jesus' ministry). The Temple cleansing is a startling action that makes clear that the new thing Christ brings will challenge and transform the old. And just as the "sign" Jesus performs at Cana occurs "on the third day"—the day of resurrection—so, too, the Temple account ends with a prophecy of his resurrection (John 2:17–22).

The first "sign" in John, then, which manifests Jesus' glory, appears to be a presaging of the glorious Messianic banquet to come. Whereas the book of Revelation concludes on this note ("The Spirit and the Bride say, 'Come.' And let him who is thirsty come, let him who desires take the water of life without price"; Rev 22:17), John's Gospel begins with it. And although Jesus is not himself the bridegroom in the Cana story, but a guest, there can be little doubt that there is in it an implicit allusion to his being the promised bridegroom of his people. The words of John the Baptist to his followers in the next chapter, in fact, reinforce the importance of this theme, when he refers to Jesus as the bridegroom and himself as "the friend of the bridegroom": "He who has the bride is the bridegroom; the friend of the bridegroom, who stands and hears him, rejoices greatly at the bridegroom's voice" (John 3:29). As the fifth-century bishop Cyril of Alexandria was to remark in a homily on the Wedding Feast of Cana, perceiving the symbolism: "Humanity, as is fitting, is called a bride, and the Savior the Bridegroom; divine Scripture thus taking images from the likeness of nature, to raise us up to the higher understanding of that which he said."[5]

In the story, the mother of Jesus (she is never named in John's Gospel) notices that the wine has run out. The flagons are empty, the old supply is exhausted, and so she turns to Jesus and says simply, "They have no wine." Jesus' reply to her, sounding harsh to our ears, actually draws

5. Quoted in Toal, *The Sunday Sermons of the Great Fathers*, 277, adapted.

on a rich symbolism that John uses more than once in his Gospel. Jesus answers: "Woman, what is there between you and me? My hour has not yet come." The address "Woman" should not be seen here as condescending or dismissive. In the Gospel of John, it points the reader's attention in the direction of "the woman" Eve, "the mother of all living" (Gen 2:23; 3:20), whom the early church—already reflected in John's Gospel—saw recapitulated in the mother of Jesus.[6] She might also be seen in this festive context as the image of Wisdom, which is depicted as a "woman" and a "mother" in Israel's wisdom literature. What the mother of Jesus says to the servants suggest as much: "Do whatever he tells you." These simple words of hers should, perhaps, bring Proverbs 9:1–5 to our minds: "Wisdom has built her house, she has set up her seven pillars. She has slaughtered her beasts, she has mixed her wine, she has also set her table . . . 'Come, eat of my bread and drink of the wine I have mixed.'"

Our icon, rich in its details, has one feature that should be noted in particular. In it, the bride and bridegroom of Cana sit, crowned, in the center. Mirroring them directly to their right and to the viewer's left are the mother of Jesus (who mirrors the bride) and Jesus (who mirrors the bridegroom). Jesus' mother inclines toward her son and his hand is extended toward the jars, into which three servants are pouring water and from which they will soon be drawing wine. The motif reminds us that the true bridegroom is the one who has united himself to creation by becoming flesh and who will bring about a great transformation. The water of the old dispensation will become the wine of the new. The "bride" of the Messiah will be those joined to him in covenant, among whom the mother of Jesus will take her place as the preeminent symbol. This is the Messianic banquet and "the marriage supper of the Lamb" in miniature and in prefigurement. And its counterpart will be the subject of the tenth mystery, the institution of the Lord's Supper.

6. This subject is explored at length in my book *The Woman, the Hour, and the Garden*.

The Eighth Mystery

Jesus' Teaching about the Kingdom of God

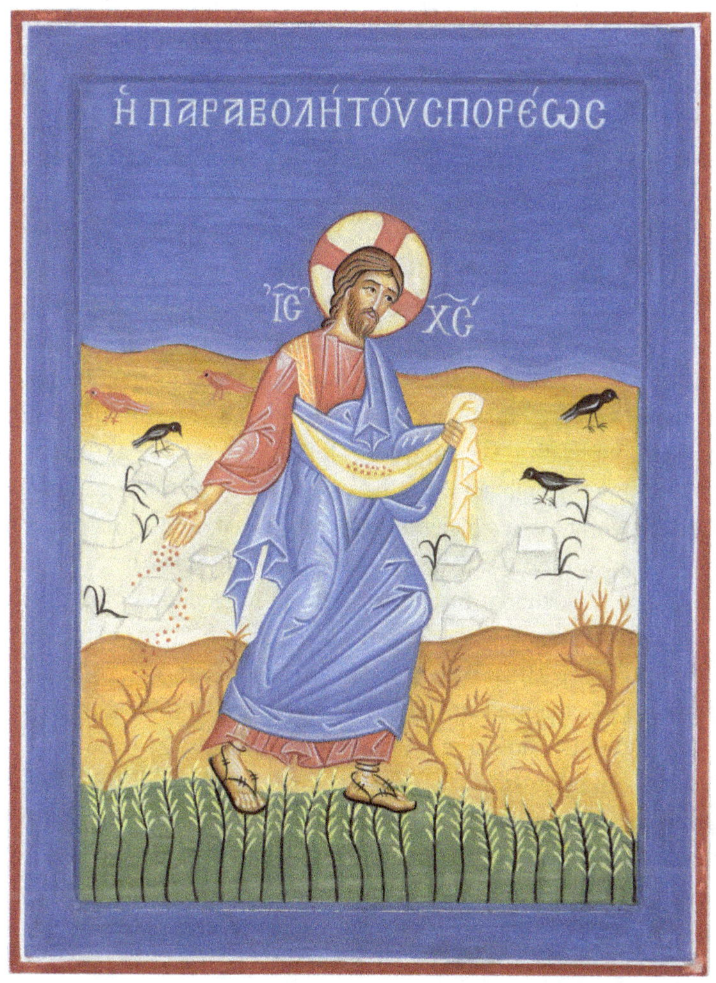

Reading for reflection:

Mark 4:1–34

For the eighth mystery we have chosen an icon depicting Jesus' parable of the Sower. This particular image, based on what truly is a seminal story that Jesus told his disciples,[7] captures something of the essence of this mystery. For the related reading, I thought it fitting to reflect on the four linked parables of Mark 4, because all four have to do with the kingdom of God, and each puts an emphasis on *hearing* and *acting upon* the teachings of Christ.

Jesus' primary mode of teaching was through parables—"he did not speak to them without a parable, but privately to his own disciples he explained everything" (Mark 4:34). A "parable" could be anything from a pithy saying to a comparison ("With what can we compare the kingdom of God . . . ?"; Mark 4:30) to a story. Jesus employed all three—pithy and witty statements, vivid comparisons and similes, and, of course, striking but simple and memorable stories. Mark indicates that he intended his parables as a challenge to his listeners to listen more closely to his words and to pursue his train of thought to arrive at understanding. He was out to make disciples, not merely converts to an abstract body of doctrine. Disciples, by definition, are learners, pupils, those committed to following a teacher and incorporating his teaching through action. When we think of Jesus as teacher—which he quite evidently saw as his chief mission—we should think of someone more like a guru than a university lecturer. His disciples literally followed him, watched him, shared his life, ate with him, listened to his words and meditated on them, and were rewarded by hearing him "explain everything in private" to them. Those who heard his strange sayings, his odd comparisons, and his unexplained stories and walked away, with no curiosity or no wish to pursue them to some fuller understanding, were—at least, for the time being—"those outside" (Mark 4:11). "The secret [literally, "mystery"—*mysterion*] of the kingdom of God," which Jesus explained in private to those inside his circle of disciples, was not for them. Those outside "may indeed see but not perceive, and may indeed hear but not understand; lest they should turn again, and be forgiven," Jesus says, according to Mark, quoting Isaiah 6:9. However we understand the import of those words (if, indeed, verse 12 is even an actual quotation of Jesus and not a Markan insertion), the point is that the parables are a boundary between those inside and those outside Jesus' circle of resolute followers. Again, Jesus was out to gather disciples, not camp followers and groupies.

The four parables in Mark 4 are about two and only two things. First, they are about "the kingdom"—or "the empire"—"of God." Jesus saw

7. Parallels to this passage are found in Matt 13:1–23; Luke 8:4–15; *The Gospel of Thomas*, logion 9.

himself as the herald of God's empire, sowing the message that, right under the nose of the Roman empire, God was establishing another kingdom. It would start out small, like a tiny mustard seed, but eventually grow to tremendous proportions (Mark 4:30–32). This particular comparison is dripping with irony and humor, because mustard bushes were not very big at all and were an invasive and not especially welcome growth. In fact, they were a nuisance. This mustard bush, however, as unwanted and invasive as it is, is guaranteed to keep growing until the birds of the air find protection in its large branches and under its capacious shade. Likewise, God's empire is unstoppable. "The kingdom of God is as if a man should scatter seed upon the ground . . . The seed produces of itself" (Mark 4:26–29). Once it takes root, it will progress relentlessly until the harvest finally comes—"first the blade, then the ear, then the full grain in the ear."

The kingdom of God, then, is *what* is planted, and Jesus sees his mission as one of sowing the seed of the kingdom. But the other aspect that these four parables emphasize is not just *what* is sown, but *how* it is sown. And *how* it is sown comes through the attentive *listening* Jesus' disciples are expected to give to his words. To the extent that they pay attention, learn, and put into action his teachings, can his followers be said to have received what he has sown. As they grow in their understanding, the kingdom grows within them. In that sense, the kingdom of God is a new way of life, a new way to live and operate in the world until the new age arrives. Jesus' intention is that not only are his teachings to be heard but made visible before the world through the lives—the deeds, daily behavior, and words—of his pupils. That is the meaning of his parable of the lamp, which is not supposed to be put under a "dry-goods basket"[8] or a bed, but rather in a prominent place where its light can shine out (Mark 4:21). Nothing he teaches in secret is meant to stay secret. What he explains to his disciples in private they must in time reveal to all: "For there is nothing hid, except to be made manifest; nor is anything secret, except to come to light" (4:22). But it all comes back to how they listen—the measure or amount *of listening* that they give to his words will be rewarded with an abundant return, and their understanding will expand accordingly: "Take heed what you *hear*; the measure [of hearing] you give will be the measure you get, and still more will be given you. For to him who has will more be given; and from him who has not [perhaps referring to the resultant loss of turning back

8. D. B. Hart, *The New Testament*, 70.

from a commitment to discipleship], even what he has will be taken away" (Mark 4:24-25; emphasis mine).

Having looked at these other three parables, we can see how the parable of the Sower, the seed, and the variety of soils is basic to everything else Jesus teaches in the Gospels. It takes first place as the foundational parable. In Mark's retelling of it, the very first word in the parable—"Listen!" (*Akouete*)—stresses its central concern, and the final words of it—"Let him who has ears to hear, let him hear" (*akouein akoueto*)—does the same (Mark 4:3, 9). This is also one of the few parables that includes a clear explanation. Jesus himself is, we can safely assume, the Sower (an identification explicitly made in Matthew's Gospel in an explanation of another, similar parable; Matt 13:37), as we see him depicted in our icon. What he sows is "the word" (4:14), and each of the soils where the seed falls—along the path and quickly gobbled up, the rocky ground where it is received at first but where it does not take root, the thorny ground where growth is choked, and finally the good soil—represent those persons who "hear" (Mark 4:15, 16, 18, 20) and respond to the word in various ways. The entire unit of these four parables, then, is about hearing and doing "the word."

Which begs the question: what is "the word" that Jesus sows and expects his followers to listen to attentively (and, because it is rendered in the Greek present tense, expected to listen to continually)? One thing is certain, it is not what is often considered to be "the gospel"—the preaching of salvation through the saving work of Christ. That occupies an essential place in Christian thought, obviously, and it constitutes the church's basic *kerygma* (proclamation) *about* the meaning of Jesus, but that is not what Jesus means by "the word" in the Gospels. Nor does it mean "the Bible." The Bible is a collection of books, some more important than others, some magnificent, some unedifying, some in need of sharp moral discernment, and so on. In liturgical churches, for instance, the tradition has always been to stand in attention only at the reading of the Gospels, but not for any of the other biblical readings. The reason is clear: Jesus' words are more important than anything else between the two covers of the Bible.

For Jesus, "the word" meant essentially this: "The proper time has been fulfilled and the Kingdom of God has drawn near; change your hearts and have faith in the good tidings" (Mark 1:15).[9] More than that, "the word" includes everything Jesus taught his disciples about *how to live* in this world. What he meant by receiving the word of "the kingdom of God" was that

9. D. B. Hart, *The New Testament*, 64.

his followers should put into practice what he taught, without excuses or second-guessing or explaining away those teachings.

Under the noses of the Romans, Jesus preached another "empire," one which was sown by word of mouth and took root in human hearts and could be seen in gradual personal and communal transformation—"Whoever does the will of God is my brother, and sister, and mother" (Mark 3:35); "Not every one who says to me, 'Lord, Lord,' shall enter the kingdom of heaven, but he who does the will of my Father who is in heaven" (Matt 7:21). The same word is being sown in receptive hearts today as it has been for two millennia. It comes to us through *listening* to Jesus' teachings, contemplating them and acting on them. This is the core of Christian spirituality: hearing the word of the Sower and letting the seed of the kingdom he sows take root and grow in us.

The Ninth Mystery

Jesus' Transfiguration on the Mountain

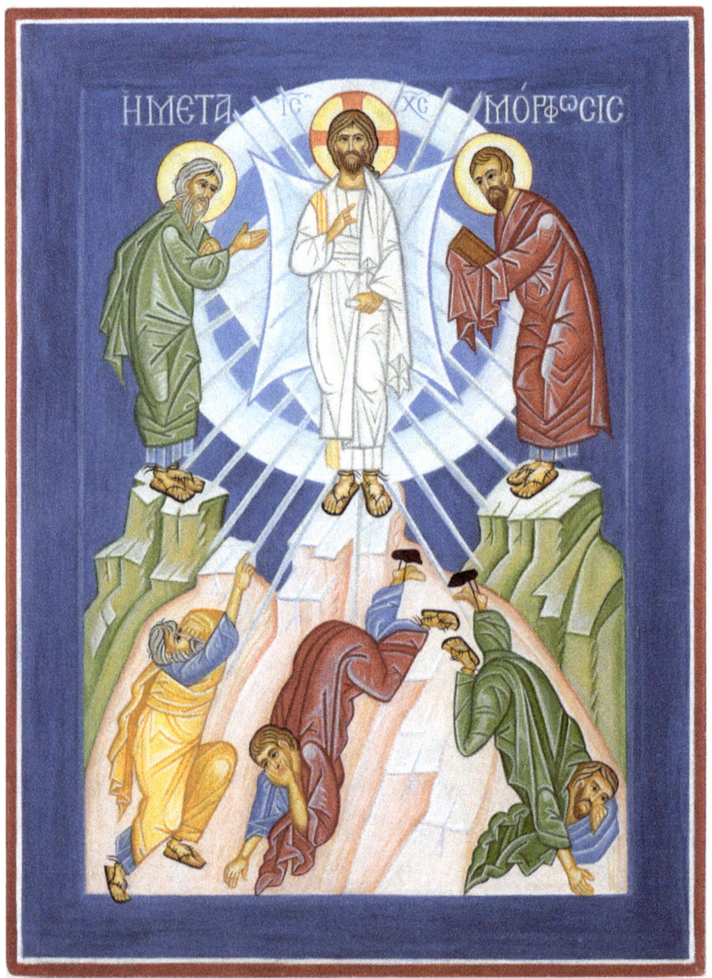

Readings for reflection:

> Mark 9:1-8; Matthew 16:28–17:8; Luke 9:27–36 (see also 2 Peter 1:16–18; 2 Corinthians 3:18–4:6)

In the ancient Middle East, mountains or high places were considered ideal locations for encounters with the sacred. In the Hebrew

Scriptures, we have two encounters that are especially significant for our ninth mystery. First, the Law was given to Moses on a mountain referred to both as Sinai and Horeb in the Pentateuch, due to the different traditions that are woven together to make up the version we have. When Yahweh made himself present there, the mountain is said to have been clothed in a shielding, glorious cloud and smoke (see Exod 19:16–20; 24:15–18; 34:5), a notable feature that will reappear again. The second relevant encounter, occurring some centuries after Moses, involves the prophet Elijah. Fleeing the wrath of King Ahab and his queen Jezebel, the prophet made his way to Mount Horeb, where in his tribulations he heard "the still small voice" of God (1 Kgs 19).

Elements of these two stories about Moses and Elijah ("the Law and the Prophets" in miniature) reappear in the Synoptic Gospels' somewhat varying accounts of the Transfiguration of Christ.[10] The Transfiguration is, of course, *the* critical mountaintop experience in those three Gospels, the "hinge" joining the early part of Jesus' ministry and the subsequent journey to the cross. In the tradition of the church, the mountain of the Transfiguration is Mount Tabor, which is located in lower Galilee at the eastern end of the Valley of Jezreel. The Gospels, however, do not name the mountain; it is enough, it seems, that it is a *mountain* on which Jesus reveals his glory. And present in the accounts is the enveloping cloud and the resplendent glory of Sinai/Horeb; and here too are Elijah and Moses, back from the beyond.

Mountains, in fact, play a significant role in all four canonical Gospels, although the roles they play vary from Gospel to Gospel. We find Jesus teaching, healing, and praying on mountains (Matt 5:1–2; 14:23; 15:29; Mark 3:13; 6:46; Luke 6:12; John 6:3, 15). In Matthew's Gospel, Jesus brings the Law and the Prophets to completion (Matt 5:17–20), so—as God gave the Law on Mount Sinai—Jesus gives his authoritative interpretation of the Torah in the form of a "Sermon *on the Mount*" (Matt 5–7). In Luke's Gospel, on the other hand, Jesus ascends mountains in order to pray. So it is that in Luke he gives a "Sermon *on the Plain*," after first descending from a mountain where he has been engaged in prayer (Luke 6:12, 17, 20).

As mentioned above, the three narratives vary in the telling of the story. In Mark's account, Jesus takes the disciples Peter, James, and John up into the heights to reveal to them "that the kingdom of God has come with power" (Mark 9:1). In Matthew, it is to reveal "the Son of Man coming in

10. For an in-depth and richly detailed study of the Transfiguration motif in Eastern Christian art and spirituality, see Nes, *The Uncreated Light*.

his kingdom" (Matt 16:28). And in Luke, it is simply a revelation of "the kingdom of God" (Luke 9:27). All three agree that the revelation on the mountain is about the kingdom of God.

In Mark and Matthew, the Transfiguration appears to be an intentional revelation so that the eyes of the disciples might be opened to a greater realization of who Jesus is and that the kingdom has come. In Luke we have a slightly different version of the event. Jesus goes "up on the mountain" primarily in order "to pray," and it is while he is praying that "the appearance of his countenance was altered, and his raiment became dazzling white" (Luke 9:27–29). In other words, as Luke describes it, Jesus is face to face with his Father on the mountain, just as Moses had been face to face with Yahweh. Jesus' disciples are bystanders looking on. Moses's encounter had resulted in the unearthly shining of his face—a lingering, but fading, reflection of divine glory (Exod 34:29–35). In Jesus' case, though, his shining countenance is not the reflection of a fading divine glory from without, but he is the source of the resplendence itself shining from within. Whereas in Luke Jesus faces the Father in prayer and, while so doing, is transfigured, in Mark and Matthew he purposely faces his disciples and directly manifests his glory to them.

While Matthew, Mark, and Luke agree that Moses and Elijah appeared with the transfigured Christ, Luke alone adds the detail that they "spoke of his *exodus* which he was to accomplish at Jerusalem." Clearly, the presence of Moses takes priority over Elijah's for both Matthew and Luke. In Luke this is highlighted by his use of the weighted word *exodus* to describe the coming events of Jesus' passion, death, and resurrection, hearkening back to the story of Moses.

Mark, the oldest of the Gospels, saw the significance of these two visitors differently. This is seen in how he stresses the appearance of Elijah over that of Moses: "And there appeared to them Elijah, with Moses." Moses is in the secondary place. Probably this is because Mark links this appearance of Elijah, who is in spirit associated with John the Baptist, to the question the disciples ask Jesus as they descend the mountain following the Transfiguration. Knowing their traditions regarding the Messiah and the prophecies of Malachi (Mal 4:5–6, LXX; 3:23–24, Masoretic Text), they ask Jesus, "Why do the scribes say that first Elijah must come?" (Mark 9:11). For Mark, Elijah has already come figuratively in John the Baptist, but—in the Transfiguration—he has also come in his own person. Moses's presence, while significant, is of lesser importance to Mark.

While noting these narrative details, it is also important to recognize a conventional pattern in the structure of the account. The Transfiguration is among a handful of revelatory moments that closely resemble one another and share a discernible "shape." One of these is found in Daniel 10:2–10. In that passage, Daniel is met by a man of whom it is said that "his face [was] like the appearance of lightning, his eyes like flaming torches," and so on. The men who accompany Daniel, we are told, "did not see the vision," but the seer himself is so overcome with fear that he falls on his face to the ground. "And behold," the text continues, "a hand touched me and set me trembling on my hands and knees." Similar to this encounter in Daniel is the conversion of St. Paul on the road to Damascus, recounted three times—each time more elaborately—in the book of Acts (9:1–9; 22:6–16; 26:12–18). There Jesus appears in brilliant, blinding light. Paul and his companions fall to the ground, though his companions only hear the voice but do not see Jesus as Paul does. Jesus exhorts Paul to get up and then proceeds to give him directions. A third example of this same pattern is found in the opening chapter of the book of Revelation (1:12–18). John on Patmos turns, upon hearing a voice behind him, and beholds the risen Jesus in much the same semblance as "the man" in Daniel 10, "his eyes like a flame of fire . . . his face like the sun shining in full strength." "When I saw him," says John, "I fell at his feet as though dead." And also, as in Daniel 10, there is the significant "touch," accompanied by an exhortation not to be afraid: "But he laid his right hand upon me, saying, 'Fear not.'" In all three of these examples we have the brilliant light, the fearful falling to the ground, and the subsequent raising up from it—which, in Daniel and Revelation, is accompanied with a touch of the hand.

The Transfiguration accounts fit this recognizable pattern, but what is revealed is more remarkable than what we find in these other biblical accounts. For one thing, in none of them do we have the apparent transformation of a human person into, in effect, a heavenly being. Whereas with Daniel's vision, "the man" who appears to him is clearly otherworldly in origin, here the one who is transfigured is the disciples' flesh and blood teacher. And whereas Paul in Acts and John in Revelation see variations of the risen and glorified Christ, the three disciples in the Gospels are seeing a metamorphosis of Jesus before his death occurs. With Jesus, we are led to understand, the kingdom of God and the coming age have already dawned. The two ages, present and future, have interpenetrated. The kingdom is present in a hidden and dynamic way, but it has yet to be seen in all its fullness. In Jesus' metamorphosis, though, something of that splendor is glimpsed, flanked by the representatives of Israel's Law and the Prophets.

With Jesus' transfiguration comes the sudden overshadowing by the "bright cloud" and the thunderous voice "borne to him by the Majestic Glory": "This is my beloved Son, with whom I am well pleased; listen to him!" (see 2 Pet 1:18; Matt 17:5) Overcome with dread before the resplendent face of Christ and the other manifestations of divine power, Peter, James, and John fall like tenpins to the ground in terror, as we see depicted in our icon. At this point, and only in Matthew's account, there then occurs the moment of the reassuring "touch," as in the book of Daniel and Revelation: "Jesus came and touched them, saying, 'Rise, and have no fear.' And when they lifted up their eyes, they saw no one but Jesus only" (Matt 17:7–8).

Much more could be said about the Transfiguration and its meaning, but there is one strand of its significance that remains relevant for followers of Jesus in their daily practice. The Transfiguration not only revealed who Christ is by nature, but also what Jesus' disciples are becoming by the inner working, usually imperceptible, of his Spirit (or "Breath"): "And we all, . . . beholding the glory of the Lord, are being transfigured into his likeness from one degree of glory to another" (2 Cor 3:18; the word *transfigured* in this text—*metamorphoumetha*—is the same as that used for Jesus' transfiguration on the mount). The revelation of the transfigured Christ is meant to abide in our minds as a promise that the kingdom of God has come and dwells within us: "For it is the God who said, 'Let light shine out of darkness,' who has shown in our hearts to give the light of the knowledge of the glory of God in the face of Christ" (2 Cor 4:6).

Although it was not for Peter, James, and John at that time to abide on the mountain and continue to behold the glorified Christ, we can resort there in spirit as often as we need. Jesus then had his "exodus" yet to undergo, for which his disciples were still unprepared. But that exodus was to be short-lived, and on the third day it was accomplished. Risen and glorified, we are continually called to recognize in his countenance "the glory of God" in our meditations—something that our icon can help us to do on a basic level. More profoundly still, his features are to be sought within ourselves, so that we too might be transfigured.

The Tenth Mystery

The Institution of the Lord's Supper

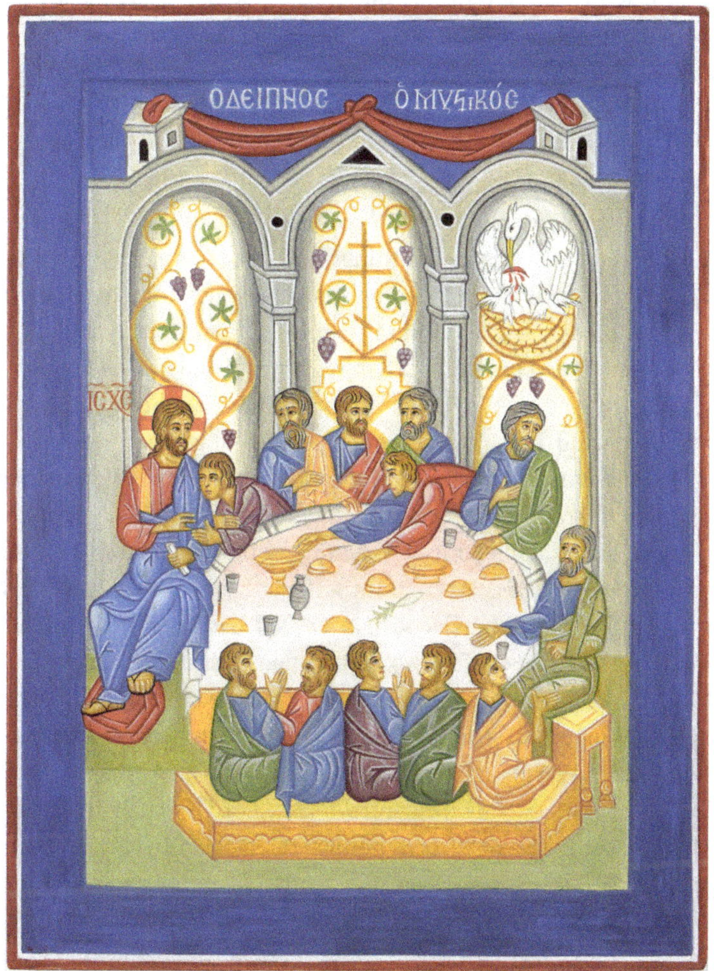

Readings for reflection:

> Mark 14:17–26; Matthew 26:20–30; Luke 22:14–39; 1 Corinthians 10:16–17, 21; 11:17–34; John 6:51-66

To appreciate the meaning and purpose of the Eucharist in the life of the church it is helpful to have some rudimentary knowledge of the interrelationship of covenant, sacrifice, and the sacrificial meal in ancient Middle Eastern culture. That is where the sacrament's roots lie, and if anything should remind Christians that their religion is eastern Mediterranean in origin it is the celebration of "the Lord's Supper." At its most basic, of course, the Eucharist is a "meal," a "supper." This in itself is significant. Meal-sharing in the Middle Eastern culture of Jesus' day (and still in many places today) usually involved partaking from the same dishes and was an implicit sign of fellowship and unity. Those who ate together were bound together. Meals had a significance greater than merely being fed, in other words, often ensuring solidarity and community.

So it was that there were few things held to be morally more despicable than an act of betrayal perpetrated by someone with whom one had shared the table. We see this way of thinking expressed, for example, in Psalm 41:9 (which is even quoted in John 13:18 in reference to Judas): "Even my bosom friend in whom I trusted, who ate of my bread, has lifted his heel against me." Betrayal after bread, it was considered, is as low as it gets.

We also see in the Hebrew Scriptures that a solemn covenantal agreement between two parties frequently involved sacrifice followed by a sacrificial meal. For example, one can see this in the covenant that those two consummate con artists, Jacob and his Uncle Laban, established between themselves (Gen 31). After Jacob had fleeced Laban and then fled from him, only to be overtaken, the two men settled their differences by "cutting a covenant." Laban suggested that an agreement be struck: "Come now, let us make a covenant, you and I; and let it be a witness between you and me" (Gen 31:44). The terms having been made, Laban then underscored the weightiness of any breach of the contract: "The Lord watch between you and me, when we are absent one from another" (Gen 31:49). This last statement, it must be noted, is not a greeting card sentiment, although (ludicrously) it has sometimes been used as such. It is, on the contrary, a warning with an implied threat attached—God will judge severely the one who violates the covenant. "See this heap [of stones] and the pillar, which I have set [as a boundary marker] between you and me," says Laban to Jacob. "This heap is a witness, and the pillar is a witness, that I will not pass over this heap to you, and you will not pass over this heap and this pillar to me, for harm" (Gen 31:51–52). After this, the covenant between them was "cut," that is to say, an animal was slain. This action meant that if either party broke the terms of the covenant the violator could likewise expect to be "cut"—slain like the sacrificial animal. After that, the sacrificial meal was eaten by both parties:

"Jacob offered a sacrifice on the mountain and called his kinsmen [Laban and those with him] to eat bread" (Gen 31:54).

In this story we see a basic outline of covenant-making, with its features of sacrifice and sacrificial meal, and a warning regarding betrayal. It is essentially the same "shape" found in the establishing of the covenant between God and the Israelite "assembly" (Heb., *qahal*; in Greek, *ekklesia*, or "church") in Exodus 24. At the foot of Mount Sinai, Moses offers sacrifice, using the blood, the symbol of life itself, to consecrate the altar and the people. The covenant agreement is made on the terms set by God in his commandments, and the people in turn promise to live accordingly: "Then [Moses] took the book of the covenant, and read it in the hearing of the people; and they said, 'All that the LORD has spoken we will do, and we will be obedient.' And Moses took the blood and threw it upon the people, and said, 'Behold the blood of the covenant which the LORD has made with you in accordance with all these words'" (Exod 24:3–8). This is then followed by a covenant meal on Mount Sinai, the chief men of Israel accompanying Moses for the extraordinary encounter: "They beheld God, and ate and drank" (Exod 24:11).

And this is the "shape" of the Christian sacramental meal, as well. Christ is, like Moses, the mediator of a "new covenant," being both—according to Christian belief—the incarnation of the divinity with whom the covenant is made, and also the perfect and final sacrifice. He is, in whatever way his presence in the meal is understood (and it is understood in different ways in different churches—differences that are not our concern here), the sacrificial meal and spiritual sustenance of the "assembly" of his people. Through this sacrificial meal, bread and wine convey to those who receive them the sacrificed "body and blood" (or, to use the even more obviously sacrificial language of John's Gospel, the "flesh and blood") of the crucified and resurrected Jesus (1 Cor 10:16–17; John 6:51–58). That this definitive and sufficient sacrifice, completed once and for all on Calvary, was extended through all ages and made accessible in all places under the sun by the ascended Lord was believed by all Christians, and the Lord's Supper was the sacrificial meal that bound Jesus' assembly together in covenant.

We can see this indicated in our icon by the symbols which Solrunn has added. Over the table of covenantal fellowship, we see the vine and bunches of grapes, indicating that Jesus, "the true vine" (John 15:1), offers his blood under the form of wine. In the center is a stylized cross, pointing to the actual place of sacrifice itself. And to our right is the ancient symbol of the pelican feeding her young with her own blood—a visual metaphor for Jesus' self-giving care for his church.

It is Paul's account of the institution of the Eucharist, however, that puts a focus on the gravity of the covenant. After warning the Corinthian Christians that they could not be partakers (*koinonoi*) in the table of the Lord's body and blood and also partakers in pagan temple feasts (1 Cor 10:16–17, 21), constituting in effect a violation of covenant conditions, he turns his attention in 1 Corinthians 11 to the matter of disharmony among believers who were partaking in the sacrificial meal together. Paul zeroes in on the seriousness of violating what the covenant meal establishes by alluding to Judas's betrayal, who had also partaken of the Lord's Supper and afterwards betrayed Jesus: "For I received from the Lord what I also delivered to you, that the Lord Jesus, *on the night when he was betrayed*, took bread" (1 Cor 11:23). The phrase which I have italicized above has passed into most eucharistic liturgies and, because of its familiarity, is barely noticed as a result. It is, though, important to remember that Paul was not writing a liturgical text but addressing the problem of disunity within a Christian community. When he described that particular night as the one on which the Lord *was betrayed*, he was making a hard, tough, sharp-edged point. And the point was that, just as Judas had violated the covenant immediately after participating in the sacrificial meal (remember Ps 41:9!), Christians participating in the Eucharist without critical awareness could do the same.

This is why Paul could say, following the Greek text, "Whoever, therefore, eats the bread and drinks the cup of the Lord in an unworthy manner will be guilty of the body and blood of the Lord . . . For anyone who eats and drinks without discerning the body eats and drinks judgment upon himself" (1 Cor 11:27, 29). To be "guilty of the body and blood of the Lord" means, quite straightforwardly, to betray him. It is, in other words, to repeat the action of Judas. In Corinth, the inability to "discern the body" meant an inability to recognize that one is in covenant with all who share in the body of Christ, and that within that body no classes can exist. All are equal. Paul means by "body" here both the sacrament itself and the reality which participation in the sacrament makes binding: the unity and life of the church. In 1 Corinthians 12 he would go on to write at length about the church as "the body," and in chapter 10 he had already stressed that the sacrificial meal binds together that body: "Because there is one bread, we who are many are one body, for we all partake of the one bread" (1 Cor 10:17).

The Corinthian Christians failed to realize that every time they ate the sacred meal together, they were renewing their baptismal covenant with both Christ and their fellow disciples. They were binding themselves through Christ to one another. To mistreat each other, to gossip about each other, to create divisions between rich and poor, to break the moral laws established by God, and so on, was to violate the covenant. It was, in effect, to repeat the action of Judas, becoming "guilty of the body and blood of the Lord" as he had. Instead of receiving grace and redemption through the sacrament, as one ought, Paul says boldly that one receives "judgment." It is the same Christ who is received in the meal, but—so Paul indicates—he can be received either as Savior or as Judge. It is the nature of the covenant that makes viable both possibilities. To use the later language of Catholic sacramental theology, the efficacy of the sacrament depends on the disposition of the one receiving it.

However, Paul, as ever, emphasizes grace, not judgment. "Let a man examine himself," he writes, "and so eat of the bread and drink of the cup" (1 Cor 11:28). That is to say, the Lord *wants* his disciples at his table—his desire is that they take their rightful places and together, as one body, receive the grace he offers. "If we judge ourselves truly," Paul writes encouragingly, "we should not be judged" (1 Cor 11:31). Paul is clear that this is a freely bestowed covenant of redemption and healing, which the sacrificial meal makes binding. As the second of the three eucharistic exhortations in *The Book of Common Prayer*—designed to be read aloud to Anglican congregations by their parish priests—put the matter: "[I]n God's behalf, I bid you all that are here present; and beseech you, for the Lord Jesus Christ's sake, that ye will not refuse to come thereto, being so lovingly called and bidden by God himself . . . I exhort you, as ye love your own salvation, that ye will be partakers of this holy Communion."[11]

One of the best-loved poems of George Herbert was perhaps even inspired by this invitation in the English Prayer Book. It reminds us with clarity that the greatest guiding principle of life in Christ is meant to be that of loving grace. We are, our failings acknowledged, our imperfections notwithstanding, urged to start anew on the road regularly. That regular reminder comes to us in the form of a shared meal and an exhortation to take, eat, and drink, which in turn is the enduring reminder of God's inclusive grace and love toward us. So, I conclude here with Herbert's magnificent poem:

11. *Book of Common Prayer*, 150–51.

Love bade me welcome: yet my soul drew back,
    Guilty of dust and sin.
But quick-eyed Love, observing me grow slack
    From my first entrance in,
Drew nearer to me, sweetly questioning
    If I lacked anything.

"A guest," I answered, "worthy to be here":
    Love said, "You shall be he."
"I, the unkind, ungrateful? Ah, my dear,
    I cannot look on thee."
Love took my hand, and smiling did reply,
    "Who made the eyes but I?"

"Truth, Lord; but I have marred them; let my shame
    Go where it doth deserve."
"And know you not," says Love, "who bore the blame?"
    "My dear, then I will serve."
"You must sit down," says Love, "and taste my meat."
    So I did sit and eat.

(*Love [III]*, 1633)

Third Set: The "Sorrowful" Mysteries

Kenosis

The Eleventh Mystery

Jesus in the Garden of Gethsemane

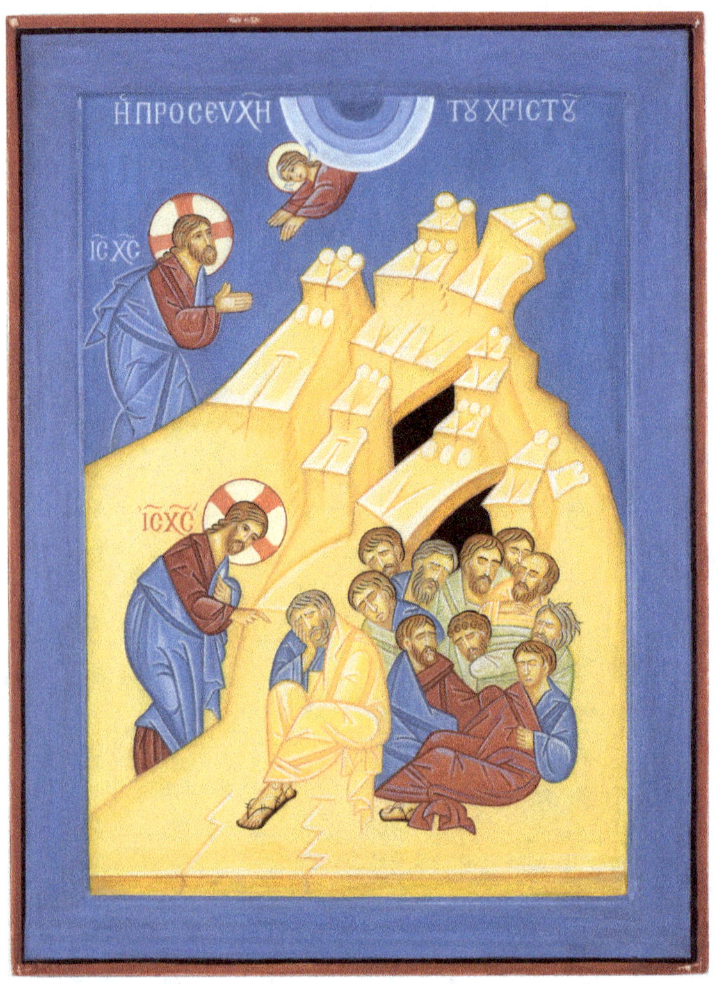

Readings for reflection:

> Mark 14:26–50; Matthew 26:30–56; Luke 22:39–54; John 18:1–13; Hebrews 5:7–10

As with some of the previous mysteries we have discussed that are derived from more than one Gospel (the baptism of Jesus, the

Transfiguration), the differences between the various accounts of Jesus' prayer and arrest in Gethsemane are enlightening. Each of the Gospels interprets the event according to its understanding of who Jesus is—in other words, according to its Christology. There is some distance in perspectives between the oldest canonical Gospel's—Mark's—account and John's. In the Synoptics, Jesus' humanity and vulnerability are fully on display. In John's account, we see no vulnerability on Jesus' part; indeed, the power of his divinity overwhelms his captors, causing them to fall to the ground. That the early church held these Gospels together in evident tension was bold, to say the least, since there was no disguising the fact that there were even contradictions between them (as we will see in one notable place). Apparently, this did not bother the earliest generations as much as it has later ones on occasion—so much so that discrepancies have often been flatly and dogmatically denied. After all, for the early Christians, their tradition held together the daringly contradictory claim that, in Jesus, we see joined both full humanity and absolute deity. The Synoptics and John, then, could be regarded as united in a sort of yin-and-yang complementarity, rather than as standing in stark contrast. Still, we need to look briefly, but seriously, at the differences we find in the texts.

Mark and Matthew are the closest in their descriptions of the scene, the latter merely reworking Mark's narrative. In their shared account, Jesus is so distressed that he falls facedown to pray. He confesses his misery to his disciples in these striking words: "My soul is very sorrowful, even to death" (Mark 14:34; Matt 26:38; meaning, in effect, "I am so distraught that I could die"). These are the words of a suffering human being, as is the plea he makes to the Father: "Abba, Father, all things are possible to thee; remove this cup from me; yet not what I will, but what thou wilt" (Mark 14:36; see Matt 26:39 and Luke 22:42). We should note here that Jesus is saying that his own (human) will differs from the Father's. The great difficulty for him in the Synoptics at this point is *obedience*—he wants to avoid what is coming, but he knows he cannot. He must go through with the ordeal. This struggle in the heart of Jesus in Gethsemane is mentioned obliquely in Hebrews 5:7–8: "In the days of his flesh, Jesus offered up prayers and supplications, with loud cries and tears, to him who was able to save him from death, and he was heard for his godly fear. Although he was a Son, *he learned obedience* through what he suffered" (emphasis added). The author of Hebrews is not suggesting that Jesus was ever disobedient, but that his obedience was made complete in its acceptance of death. And Jesus "was heard," says the author of Hebrews—an assertion seemingly congruent with one of the two verses in Luke's account that do not appear in all ancient texts of that Gospel, but which immediately follow his prayer of resignation and supply an answer to it: "And there appeared to him an angel from heaven, strengthening him" (Luke 22:43).

Luke's account truncates all this. Most noticeably, Jesus does not fall prostrate to the ground, but rather kneels to pray. He says nothing about feeling distress, but instead cautions his disciples to pray that they "enter not into temptation" (Luke 22:40). The second of the two verses (22:44) that does not appear in all ancient texts, tells us that Jesus was "in an agony" and that "his sweat became like great drops of blood falling down upon the ground." The word *agonia*—"agony"—does not mean "pain" or inner torment, but rather "struggle." In other words, Jesus is in some sort of interior wrestling match. But, with verses 43–44 in dispute and usually not included in our translations, we are left in Luke with a relatively less intense picture of Jesus' prayer in Gethsemane than we find in Mark and Matthew. He prays only once, for example, not three times as in the other two Synoptics.

When we read of the arrest in the Synoptics, we see that Matthew has added to Mark's shorter version. In Matthew, Jesus' concealed authority is insinuated. When the ear of the slave of the high priest is severed "by one of those" who accompanies Jesus, he responds in Matthew's account with these words, indicating that everything is really under divine control: "Put your sword back into its place; for all who take the sword will perish by the sword. Do you think that I cannot appeal to my Father, and he will at once send me more than twelve legions of angels? But how then should the scriptures be fulfilled, that it must be so?" (Matt 26:52–54). In Luke's account, he is even more in charge. There, he heals the slave's ear after saying commandingly to those around him: "No more of this!" (Luke 22:51). And, as he gives himself over to those arresting him, he says, "But this is your hour [meaning a period of limited duration], and the power of darkness" (Luke 22:53).

But it is in John's account, as we might expect, where we see the greatest departure. For one thing, only John refers to the place as a "garden" (John 18:1)—Mark and Matthew refer to it as "Gethsemane" ("Oil Press")—and when we see the word *garden* in John we are meant to see in it an implicit reference to Eden (so it is that Jesus' death and resurrection are associated with a garden; John 19:41; 20:15). Second, Jesus does not pray in the garden. He has just prayed, on the other side of the Kidron valley, what has been called "the high priestly prayer" (John 17 in its entirety), which consisted in an affirmation of his divine status, a prayer for the restoration of his eternal glory, and prayers for his disciples. There is no distress, no sorrow, no prostration, no agony in John. Instead, as we remarked above, there is a demonstration of his power. He is in charge of the situation when he is arrested, twice demanding of those who have come to take him, "Whom do you seek?" The first time that they answer, "Jesus of Nazareth," we are told that he said to them, "I am he" (literally, *I am*—the name of God given to Moses in Exodus 3:13–14) and immediately "they drew back and fell to the ground." Only after he has identified himself a second time—and the reader is meant to understand that he has actually identified himself as YHWH, "I Am"—and secured his disciples' release, does he hand himself over to the guard. Smaller details also differ from the Synoptic accounts. John identifies the slave of the high priest by name (Malchus) and tells us that the one who struck off his ear was Peter. Nor does Judas identify Jesus to his captors with a kiss. All in all, we have a strikingly different atmosphere surrounding his arrest in the fourth Gospel.

Perhaps most striking of all is the direct contradiction between Jesus' plea in the Synoptics for the Father to take away the cup of suffering and Jesus' almost strident acceptance of it in John: "Jesus said to Peter, 'Put your sword into its sheath; shall I not drink the cup which the Father has given me?'" (John 18:11) Even earlier than this, John had presented Jesus as saying these words (and, in this instance, acknowledging his inner distress): "Now is my soul troubled. And what shall I say, 'Father, save me from this hour'? No, for this purpose I have come to this hour" (John 12:27). Here we see no need on Jesus' part "to learn obedience"—he is, despite his anxiety, prepared to meet his sufferings. He has no intention of crying out to the Father to take away the terrible cup.

So, what are we to make of this yin-and-yang picture of the scene in Gethsemane as presented to us in the canon—on the one hand, the fully human Jesus, crying out to his Father to be spared from his coming suffering and death, distraught and depressed and lying prostrate on the ground or kneeling in supplication; on the other hand, the God-man, fully in control of the situation, bowling over his captors with the power of his word, and only permitting his arrest on his own terms? As we said above, the church boldly kept these two very different takes on the same event together, not dispensing with one or the other for the sake of a flat, lifeless consistency. One might accuse the early Christians of being woolly-minded for doing so. For that matter, the tradition's insistence that in Jesus' person we find a similar yin and yang of human and divine natures is likewise confounding—nor is it ever in the tradition satisfyingly (at least, to our system-fabricating minds) explained in a way, even in the most thorough historical christological clarifications, that does not still leave us with an apparent logical antinomy. If ever there were a Zen-like dogma of the faith, it is this one. Sticking with our yin-and-yang analogy, we can suggest that, if we look "into" the tradition underlying the Synoptic Gospels (as perhaps the author of Hebrews had) we might see Christ's divine sonship after all; and if we look "into" the Johannine text, we will not fail to note the human nature of the Word-made-flesh ("Now is my soul troubled . . ."). And Zen-like, we should just take this apparent logic-busting conundrum as it is presented to us into our meditation.

In our own lives, we can fully identify with the anguish of Jesus in Gethsemane because, in it, he is identified with us. The same author of Hebrews reassures his readers along these lines: "For we have not a high priest who is unable to sympathize with our weaknesses, but one who in every respect has been tempted [or 'tested'] as we are, yet without sin [or 'without going off-course']" (Heb 4:15). By the same token, we can—at least, occasionally—recognize in ourselves the power of God at work, giving us the grace we require: "Let us then with confidence draw near to the throne of grace, that we may receive mercy and find grace to help in time of need" (Heb 4:16). Rather than attempt to explain these things to ourselves rationally, we should instead endeavor to quiet our restless thoughts, enter within the Gethsemane of our own "hearts," and encounter Christ there.

The Twelfth Mystery

The Scourging of Jesus

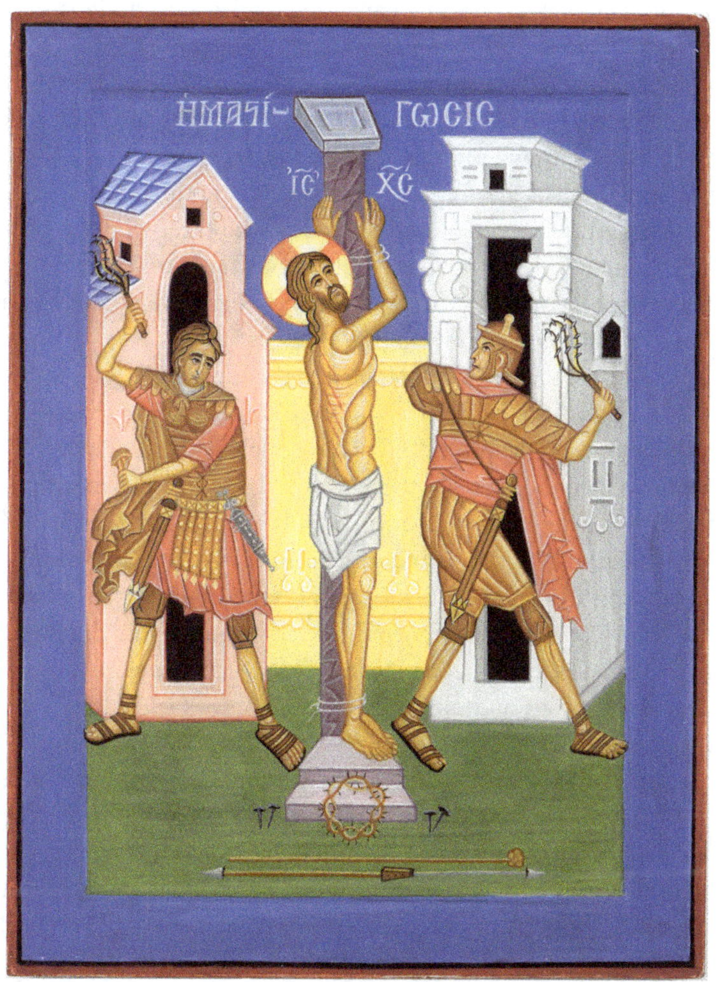

Readings for reflection:

Mark 15:15; Matthew 27:26; John 19:1

Although there are traditions of affective spirituality in the Western church, both Catholic and Protestant, which put imaginative stress on Jesus' sufferings, one finds no effort on the part of the four Evangelists to evoke readers' affectivity regarding them. Each of the Gospels, despite the differences between them, tends to tell its version of the Passion Narrative (and everything else besides) straightforwardly, with little or no graphic detail. We find in them no extended descriptions of Jesus' sufferings like those, for example, we read in the more explicit accounts of suffering and martyrdom in 2 Maccabees 6 and 7 (and retold, with even more detail, in 4 Maccabees). As the reader can see in the texts cited above, for the scourging of Jesus we have just three verses to go on—one from each of three of the Gospels—and they say nothing beyond the fact that he was scourged by the Roman soldiers. The three who mention it—Mark, Matthew, and John—appear reticent to say more about it than is absolutely necessary. And Luke says nothing whatsoever about either the scourging of Jesus or his crowning with thorns.

Why is there so little attention paid to the specifics of Jesus' sufferings on the part of the Evangelists? Certainly, in Western religious art from the high Middle Ages to the present there has not been any hesitancy to depict them. Still, as mentioned above, there grew up in the Latin West an affective spirituality—one that engaged the senses and the emotions. We see the budding of it as early as Augustine; and with the likes of—for example—Anselm, Bernard and the Cistercians and those they inspired, and later still with Francis and the movement he engendered, we see it coming into full flowering. There is much to admire and even to love in this affective spirituality, which gave birth to great art and spread out into numerous currents of devotion that enriched—when it was healthy—the lives of believers.

That said, for many reasons well beyond the scope of our reflections here, over time there grew up with it a not so healthy attachment to imaginative details of Jesus' agonies. More emphasis was placed on the gruesome and bloody aspects of them, with fraudulent relics and elaborate devotions to his wounds, the implements used to torture him, his blood, his tears, and so on. In some cultural contexts, artists and the makers of life-like statuary went so far as to feature his sufferings in unrelentingly gory detail. In some parts of the Catholic world, devotion to Jesus' sufferings have even led to cultic displays of self-mutilation and crucifixion. And this unwholesome stress on the gruesome aspects of the passion remains a spiritual and devotional feature to this day, even in the more "sophisticated" form of contemporary cinema. Mel Gibson's *The Passion of the Christ* was released in 2003 to much acclaim. With computerized special effects unknown to previous generations of filmmakers, Gibson was able to present us with what was roughly two hours of unrelieved sadism and brutal violence. And one of the most repellent, drawn out, and—frankly—pointless scenes was the one depicting the scourging of Christ, a scene awash in blood and strewn with chunks of mutilated flesh by the end. And all that was based on three, short, flatly stated parallel verses in the Gospels.[1]

And yet, in defense of Gibson and others who would portray Christ's sufferings "realistically," one might argue (and it has been argued), wasn't this precisely what Jesus went through "for our sakes"? Shouldn't it be put out there before our eyes in all its undeniable ugliness? Is it right that we shield ourselves from the full horror of it? The early Christians, after all, knew what Roman scourging and the Roman "science" of crucifixion looked like. Shouldn't we stifle our squeamishness, "get real," and look at it directly?

To this, I would argue that the answer is—at least, to a great extent—probably not. We do not need to see the full extent of the torments inflicted on Jesus to understand its horror. There is a good argument to be made for exercising restraint when we depict the sacred (sacred art should always be "chaste," and the idolatry of the gruesome holds more unconscious appeal for us than we might suppose). There is also a good argument to be made for restraint in depicting scenes of abuse. Victims deserve their dignity. The obscene and dehumanizing and the details of abuse are best left to implication and suggestion and succinct statement. Exploiting the details is to exploit the victim of abuse, and that should not be indulged. As we should be aware, our human taste for the unsavory and violent is not the best characteristic of our species. And an over-emphasis on the hideousness of Jesus' torments can be, to say it straight, just another form of barely disguised prurience. It is more mentally and emotionally hygienic for us if we imitate the reticence of the Gospels.

Which is what Eastern iconography does. It dispenses intentionally with the affectively evocative, resists overstatement, and reduces the depiction to the essentials. It exists to raise the mind to contemplation, not to urge it toward emotionalism. The latter can be a cheap substitute for contemplative prayer, which is not to say that contemplative prayer rejects healthy emotion. But it does reject irrational (because it is at odds with the *logos*) emotional*ism*. We begin, of course, with the honest acknowledgment that

1. I am not arguing against depictions of violence in cinema, let it be said. I am not advocating prudery or elevating squeamishness to a virtue. I am, though, arguing that mixing elements of "Gothic horror" with an unsubtle attempt to elicit devotional feelings is alien to classical Christian spiritual practice.

life involves suffering, and we must—because we will, without exception—need to look at it. Here Christians are fundamentally in agreement with the Buddha. From there we also are impelled to see clearly and logically that Jesus' sufferings were not unusual or more painful or more horrible than the sufferings endured by countless others. That, despite so many devotional sentiments that would say otherwise. *What Christians are supposed to note about Jesus' sufferings is not that they are unusual or absolutely unique or unexcelled, but rather that Jesus is God joined to and immersed in the suffering of all humanity and, by extension, all creation.* The suffering, then, is redemptive in nature. The promised resurrection will invert everything; the hope it generates being that through suffering—which everyone and everything endures to greater or lesser extent—we will emerge into the fullness of life. In our icon, then, we see the Roman soldiers and the cords of their spiked whips, we see Jesus' back bloodied as he stands bound to the pillar, and we see the devices associated with the passion—nails, spear, the sponge of vinegar on its pole, and the crown of thorns—at the base of the pillar. (I should mention here that Solrunn has been careful to render the soldiers and their implements in accurate historical detail, which is not often the case in classical iconography.) We are strongly put in mind of his sufferings, but through a circumspect balance of depiction and symbol, and these features move us to reflect on the *meaning* of the event rather than on the grisly particulars that a more realistic representation would force on our minds. Prurience is a temptation, but it is at odds with both meaning and contemplation. If we wish to contemplate, we will resist the temptation. And the *meaning* of his sufferings, in Christian thought, embraces us all.

If we would draw effective truth from our reflections on the abuse Jesus endured, perhaps it might be this: that Jesus, for the Christian, is "God with us." He became fully human, and in so doing he identifies with all the sufferings of humanity. Wherever persons are abused by oppressive governments, ideologues, and soulless bureaucracies; wherever people are cruelly treated, tortured, imprisoned, forced to become refugees; wherever the innocent especially are wronged, tormented, exploited, aborted, murdered; wherever people are hungry, thirsty, naked, cold, sick, frightened, disenfranchised, molested, neglected, unwanted strangers—there is Jesus. There he is, scourged in them all. And we have his own word about that, which cannot be avoided with any ready excuses by those who claim to follow him but do not do as he taught. If you want to see the suffering Jesus today, read the papers, watch the news. There he is. Reflecting on Jesus' sufferings is not just about ourselves—what he suffered "for us," how his blood "saved me" (all that is fine, so long as one does not forget the neighbor). It is about the suffering, and they are around us all the time.

"I was hungry and you gave me food, I was thirsty and you gave me drink, I was a stranger and you welcomed me, I was naked and you clothed me, I was sick and you visited me, I was in prison and you came to me . . . Truly, I say to you, as you did it to one of the least of these my brothers and sisters, you did it to me" (see Matt 25:31–46).

The Thirteenth Mystery

Jesus is Crowned with Thorns

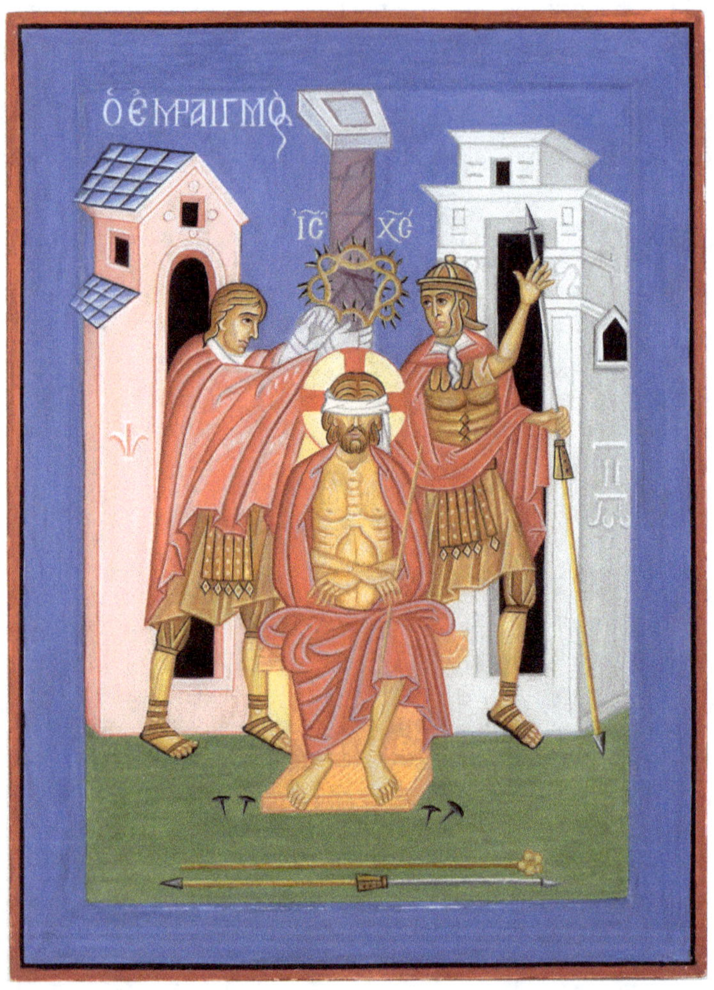

Readings for reflection:

Mark 15:16–20; Matthew 27:27–31; John 19:2–5

When the earliest generation of Greek-speaking Christians proclaimed that "Jesus is Lord" (1 Cor 12:3; Phil 2:11; see also Rom 1:3–4; 10:9–13), the political implications of that assertion would not have been far from their minds. In a world where Caesar—and Caesar alone—was proclaimed as "Lord" (and "Son of God" also), there could not in principle be room for any other "Lord." It was the emperor who stood as mediator between the divine sphere and Rome's "kingdom" (*basileia* = "empire"). And yet the earliest generation of Christians boldly declared that Jesus was "the Lord" and that they were members of God's "kingdom" (*basileia* = "empire") and of Christ's "body."

There were other terms as well that were used by the first followers of Christ in their communities that derived from common Greco-Roman political and social parlance, what we might today regard as "secular" in nature. Examples of these borrowings are: *ekklesia*, which is usually translated "church" and means literally "assembly"; *episkopos* which is usually translated "bishop" and means literally "overseer" or "supervisor"; *presbyteros*, which is usually translated "priest" and means literally "elder" or "senior"; and *diakonos*, which is usually translated "deacon" and means literally "one who serves." All of these were "secular" or non-cultic terms. Their religious, sacral associations only developed over time as the church became increasingly separated from the synagogue and began to shape its own cultic life. Even the idea of being joint-members "in the body of Christ" (or simply "in Christ")[2] was a borrowed political and social analogy—the concept of the "body politic" was a time-honored one long before Paul adapted it to describe the union of the church with its Lord and with each other.[3]

Although it is a suggestion sometimes resisted, there can be little doubt that Jesus' "movement" was consciously a political one as much as a spiritual one—if by "political" we are referring to the polity of a society. The

2. See 1 Cor 12:12–31 (and also 10:16–17; 6:13-20); Rom 12:1–10 (and also 6:1–12).

3. We find the metaphor already in use in ancient India (e.g., *Rig Veda* X, 90). The *Mahabharata* (XIV, xxii) depicts human society as originating from the body of a common ancestor—which is similar to the idea expressed by Paul in 1 Corinthians 15:22, that human beings are derived from Adam ("in Adam"). Among the Greeks, the notion of *hylozoism* (*hylo* = matter; *zoe* = life) meant that mind and life permeate the natural world. The individual human being possesses life and soul/mind, and this is in some sense identical with the one governing human-soul (*homonoia*) that animates, unifies, and guides the nation-state from the top down—that is, it moves both "the head" (the ruler) and the members of society. The ruler was also seen as "the physician" of the "body" of society. In Roman society, it was an explicitly political analogy. Livy tells of Menenius Agrippa ending a plebeian secession by explaining the nourishment of the belly (the senate) being needed for the hands and feet (common people) to function healthily (Livy, *History of Rome*, II, xxxii; compare the Greek Aesop's fable of the belly and the bodily members). The Stoics used the analogy—and Paul, who was a native of Tarsus, was reared in that most Stoic of ancient Roman cities and was certainly influenced by Stoicism.

"fellowship" (*koinonia*) of the early churches was loosely knit, but wherever communities of disciples were found its principles were recognizably rooted in Jesus' teachings. Jesus, by all accounts, had set out to form a community of love, at the heart of which was an encounter with "the Father" and an intercommunion of equality and mutual encouragement united in God's living Spirit ("Breath"). The sacraments were binding signs of this communion. If we take the parables of the kingdom as expressing the core of Jesus' gospel in story form (as he apparently did), then we should recognize that there is something subversive in them, especially in those that portray God's "empire" as growing up imperceptibly like some crop (wheat) or even like an invasive species of scrub (mustard) in the midst of Rome's flourishing empire (see our Eighth Mystery above). And Jesus announced an "empire" that inverted everything Rome understood by the term. Instead of conquest, service; instead of domination, equality and sharing; instead of violence, nonviolence; instead of strict retributive "justice," mercy and forgiveness. Jesus proclaimed an "empire" in which the "leaders" (a term he never used) were to be as humble as children and to be "slaves" to all.

When, at one point in John's Gospel, we are told that Jesus realized that the people "were about to come and take him by force to make him king," he responded by eluding them and withdrawing to a "mountain by himself" (John 6:15). Not for him the role of king or emperor (which makes the later history of Constantinianism all the more an affront to Jesus' message). And so, even as he eschewed kingship or authoritarianism for himself and his followers, Jesus' proclamation of a rival empire was almost certainly viewed as a threat to the tenuous alliance between Rome and Judea's ruling elite. We read in John that "Caiaphas, who was high priest that year, said to [the chief priests and Pharisees gathered in council], 'You know nothing at all; you do not understand that it is expedient for you that one man [Jesus] should die for the people, and that the whole nation should not perish" (John 11:49–50). What drove Caiaphas to offer this advice, John tells us, was the palpable fear that, should Jesus be allowed to "go on thus . . . the Romans [would] come and destroy" the Temple and the people (John 11:48). The declaration of the kingdom of God was perceived, it would seem, as a dangerous manifesto.

This becomes evident when we consider the "charge" against Jesus, as displayed publicly by the Roman governor. Jesus was crucified with the placarded accusation that he had proclaimed himself "the King of the Jews." Even though the Roman authorities were not likely to have understood

Jesus' message, they were not mistaken that it implied a challenge to their imperial dominance. John's Gospel in particular indicates again and again throughout its account of the passion just how provocative Jesus' proclamation of a rival kingdom was for the Romans. Did his words portend an insurrection in the works? That would have created some anxiety for the Romans policing Jerusalem during the crowded Passover season. Despite the Hollywood-inspired pictures in our heads of the events surrounding Jesus' arrest and execution, the Romans did not relish the idea of shedding blood if it could be at all avoided. So, they surely did not want an anti-Roman "king" rearing his head under such volatile circumstances. They would have agreed with Caiaphas "that one man should die [rather than] that the whole nation should perish."

And, if John's telling of the story reflects the truth of the situation, Pilate was clearly disturbed by the assertion of Jesus' "kingly" status. In the Gospel, he directly asks Jesus if he believes himself to be "the King of the Jews," to which Jesus responds, "Do you say this of your own accord, or did others say it to you about me?" (John 18:33–34). When Jesus says further that his "kingship is not from the world," Pilate picks up on the lack of denial in his words and snaps back: "So you are a king?" (18:36–37). John depicts Pilate as floundering in his understanding of what Jesus means, but he is quick to latch onto this troubling, though ambiguous, claim of "kingship" (or, more to the point, "emperorship"). A few verses later, Pilate addresses "the Judeans" apart and asks them if they prefer to see released "the King of the Jews" or Barabbas (18:39). With their choice of the latter, he hands Jesus over to the soldiers and their mockery ("Hail, King of the Jews!"; 19:3). He is "coronated" with a "crown" (*stephanon*) of thorns, arrayed in a purple robe, and repeatedly struck. Pilate, though disturbed by Jesus' words, nonetheless sees him as innocent of serious offense and seeks to release him. What forces his hand to send Jesus to the cross, though, is—according to John—the Judeans' cry: "If you release this man, you are not Caesar's friend [an honorary title]; every one who makes himself a king sets himself against Caesar" (19:12). Pilate then shows the Judeans the bloodied, "crowned" Jesus and says, as if to bring them to their senses regarding how ludicrous the charge made against this beaten and battered man is, "Behold your King!" (19:14). When they protest, he says to them, now it seems with bitter irony, "Shall I crucify your King?" To which they respond, "We have no king but Caesar" (19:15). In that protestation we hit the very nub of the Jesus problem for both Pilate and the Judean leadership:

it is about authority and empire and threats to the delicate balances of an established, but rickety, order. When Jesus is crucified, Pilate writes "a title" (*titlon*) in Hebrew, Latin, and Greek to be put on the cross that reads "Jesus of Nazareth, the King of the Jews" (19:19).

Scholars can discuss how many of these details in John are historical, embroidered, exaggerated, and so on, but one aspect rings true in this Gospel's account of the proceedings, and it is this: the claim of Jesus' kingship was one that the Romans were not about to ignore. The punishment and mockery Jesus received was directly related to claims about "the kingdom" and their implicit challenge to the authority of Rome. The brutality was directed at someone seen to be an upstart and rebel, a provocateur who needed to be taught a lesson so that, in turn, others would have an example of what happens when somebody gets too high on his horse and needs to be knocked off it. This is, after all, what empires do to those who resist their might, and Rome was never shy about reducing its enemies to nothing.

Our icon depicts Jesus, seated ("enthroned"), the purple robe around him, holding the mock scepter of a reed, and blindfolded (a detail taken from Mark 14:65 and Luke 22:64). At his feet are instruments of the passion and in the background is the pillar of the scourging. Two soldiers stand on either side of Jesus—mockeries of the cherubim who stand in God's glory and proclaim his holiness. They hold over his head the crown of thorns, with which they will cruelly "coronate" Jesus. The image depicts a violent parody of regal splendor. It is, next to the crucifixion itself, the grimmest portrayal of Jesus' *kenosis*—his self-emptying to the point of slavery, death, dehumanization, nothingness.

The icon also suggests the vast difference between the all-too-human idea of what constitutes a "kingdom" and God's kingdom. Throughout history, kingdoms and empires have been based on lies—lies about a glorious past, lies about a glorious destiny, lies about their "greatness" (all three of the above are summed up, by the way, in the motto "make America great again"). When Pilate asks Jesus, "What is truth?" and then walks out without waiting for an answer (John 18:38), he speaks as the typical mouthpiece of a cynical empire—in fact, of *any* cynical empire. "When the truth becomes legend, print the legend" (the famous and often misquoted line from *The Man Who Shot Liberty Valance*) is an iteration of the same cynical attitude. Empires build their reputations on lies about their greatness, their indispensability, their high civilizational standards, and so forth. But in fact, empires have always actually been founded and expanded (and the United States is no exception) through bloodshed, conquest, theft of territory, militarism, and slavery. What the icon of Christ humiliated and crowned with thorns shows us, in contrast to all the lies, is the stark, ugly reality of human empire. This is what empires and nations and political and military powers do to those peoples they conquer, subjugate, and enslave. Jesus is the *kenosis* of God—and in him we see God taking the side of those who are conquered, impoverished, and downtrodden by the powerful and rich. His kingship clearly is *not* of the world.

This monstrous, vicious treatment of Jesus—this image of human authoritarianism exposed for what it is—would be unbearable if not for the resurrection to come. In that event, we have the promise that human malignancy and cruelty will not have the final word. Untold manmade horrors have come and gone, and more can be expected in the future. The human animal is not fully evolved and still more bestial than beatific. But in Christ God has joined himself to human nature—even the human condition at its most damaged. The resurrection holds before us the hope that human evil will be swallowed up forever, and that humanity will reach its end which is "God all in all."

Until then, however, we must reckon with the painful reality that we are all potentially both victims and—yes—abusers of others, that human kingdoms and empires are not permanent or innately good, and that the only kingdom that will last forever is the kingdom of God (see Heb 12:25–29). Jesus is risen and glorified, but we should never forget that the only crown he ever wore on earth was a crown of thorns.

The Fourteenth Mystery

The Carrying of the Cross

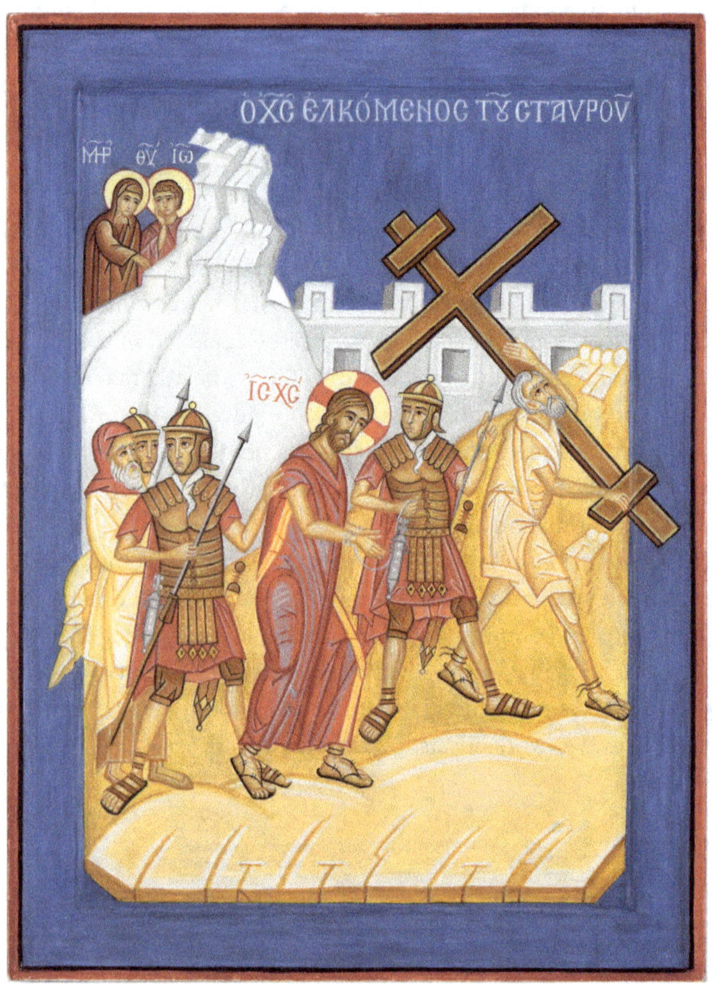

Readings for reflection:

> Mark 15:20–21; Matthew 27:31–32; Luke 23:26–32; John 19:17

The difference between the Synoptic Gospels and John's is striking where this Mystery is concerned—or it might be if it were not for the fact that centuries of tradition and numerous artistic depictions have smoothed the disparity over. In our era we have seen quite a few film versions of the life of Christ, for example, in which Simon of Cyrene is compelled by the Roman soldiers to assist the struggling Jesus carry the weight of his cross on the way to Golgotha. This is the traditional "reconstruction" of the event, combining all four accounts, and most of us are now accustomed to it. However, the first three Gospels provide us with one picture (Simon alone bears Jesus' cross) and John another (Jesus alone bears his cross).

Without the overlay of the traditional reconciling of the texts, then, we find we have an apparent contradiction. In the Synoptics, Simon from the very outset is given the task of carrying Jesus' cross (though actually only the crossbeam would have been borne), as the soldiers are just getting underway with their prisoner. Mark even provides us with a small detail about this Simon: he was "the father of Alexander and Rufus"—evidently two persons known to the community for whom Mark's Gospel was composed.[4] This aside in Mark has the ring of authenticity: Simon was evidently someone known, through his descendants, beyond his unexpected forced encounter with Jesus. Matthew and Luke omit this detail, but otherwise are faithful to Mark's version of what happened. John, on the other hand, stresses that Jesus carried "his own cross" (or carried the cross "for himself").[5] The way John phrases it comes across as an implied correction of the record. Simon, needless to say, is not mentioned by John.

Faced with this discrepancy in the canonical Gospels, the church chose to overlook it and in effect decided that both versions had it right. Jesus had carried his own cross, and also Simon had carried it, or helped him to carry it, or took over the task when it became too much for Jesus to go on. So much for a contradiction. And yet, while acknowledging all the above, perhaps the tradition's refusal to opt exclusively for one or the other

4. A long-held conjecture is that the "Rufus" mentioned here could be the same person mentioned by Paul in Romans 16:13: "Greet Rufus, eminent in the Lord, also his mother and mine." If Mark's Gospel was indeed written for the communities in Rome, as both tradition and most scholars affirm, then this is a reasonable supposition. The additional fact that Paul's Rufus is described as "eminent" and that his family—his mother—is revered by Paul lends credence to the idea. Simon or his descendants may have settled with the family in Rome and was remembered there fondly among later generations of Roman Christians, and therefore Mark (a source for the other two Synoptic Gospels, which make no mention of "Alexander and Rufus") put a focus on Simon's involvement in Jesus' final journey.

5. Possibly this is an allusion to Isaac carrying the wood to be used for his own near-sacrifice in Genesis 22:6, but this seems to be a long shot as an explanation.

has preserved two complementary meanings of the bearing of the cross. If we understand that the Gospels are not merely biographies or historical records, but that everything in them is intended to convey a deeper message for the readers, then it makes it easier for us to set aside any worries we may harbor about "contradictions" (of which there are a number, even between the Synoptics) and focus instead on the varieties of significance the authors conveyed through the literature they left to us.

Looking first at John, the latest of the four Gospels, we might note that throughout his narrative only Jesus has the power to overcome the darkness, to bear the sin of the world, and to accomplish what is, according to his message, the judgment of "this world" (John 12:31–32; see 1:29; 8:12 and parallels). In a sense other than the literal or historical one, then, nobody else can carry the cross that Jesus must carry: "For this purpose I have come to this hour" (12:27). He alone will say before succumbing to death, "It is accomplished" (19:30). In John's christology, Christ carries his life and death on his own shoulders: "I lay down my life, that I may take it again. No one takes it from me, but I lay it down of my own accord. I have power [authority] to lay it down, and I have power [authority] to take it again; this charge I have received from my Father" (10:17b–18). So, for John, it is only fitting that Jesus carries his own cross and Simon is nowhere in view. In effect, in so doing he is laying down his life.

Turning to the Synoptic Gospels, though, we have another aspect of Jesus' message highlighted precisely by Simon's bearing the cross "on the way" with Jesus. The Synoptics preserve Jesus' pre-crucifixion metaphorical saying about "the cross": "If anyone would come after me, let him deny himself and take up his cross and follow me" (Mark 8:34; see Matt 16:24; Luke 9:23). It is notable that Luke adds the word *daily*—indicating that the saying did not necessarily refer to a follower's literal martyrdom, but to a discipline or practice that was to be constant. It could be understood as a call to radical self-denial in many areas of one's life, as the rest of the passage indicates. That this metaphor of "taking up the cross" was not merely a projecting backwards onto the "historical Jesus" a post-resurrection analogy based on his own death by crucifixion is perhaps indicated by its appearance in the Gospel of Thomas, which is purely a "sayings" Gospel: "And whoever . . . will not take up his cross as I do, will not be worthy of me" (G.Thom. 55, 2). Bearing the cross is therefore a metaphor for discipleship, as is "following Jesus on the way," and—notably—Simon of Cyrene does both. It is important, it would seem, for Mark, as well as for those who used his Gospel in the composition of their own versions, that Jesus is followed by "a disciple" to the place of crucifixion. Apart from its historicity (and I believe it is historical, based on Mark's reference to Alexander and Rufus), it is symbolically potent. The disciple carries his cross and follows Christ, possibly to his own death. At all times, followers of Jesus carry their lives on their shoulders. The disciple's highest calling is to imitate the love of Christ and, in many ways, to lay down one's life for others—to forgive (meaning to "let go" and "let be" rather than to hold on to past hurts and grudges), to "love" one's enemies (which simply means to do them no harm and to be willing to do them positive good, if necessity demands), to give to those in need, to serve others, and perhaps literally to die for others.

Our icon depicts in stylized form the Synoptic version of the story. Simon carries the cross—not merely the crossbeam, but the entire symbol of the faith. He is on the way with Jesus in a sun-baked landscape, outside the city walls. Ten of the twelve disciples have fled, but we see Mary, the mother of Christ, and John, the beloved disciple, looking on and following from a distance. The historical Simon of Cyrene may have had no idea what was going on or even who Jesus was, or maybe he had. But, irrespective of that, here he symbolizes walking in the way with Jesus, fulfilling the call on the lives of all who would (in spirit) take up the cross and follow him. This is, we could say then, the icon of discipleship.

The Fifteenth Mystery

Jesus' Crucifixion and Death

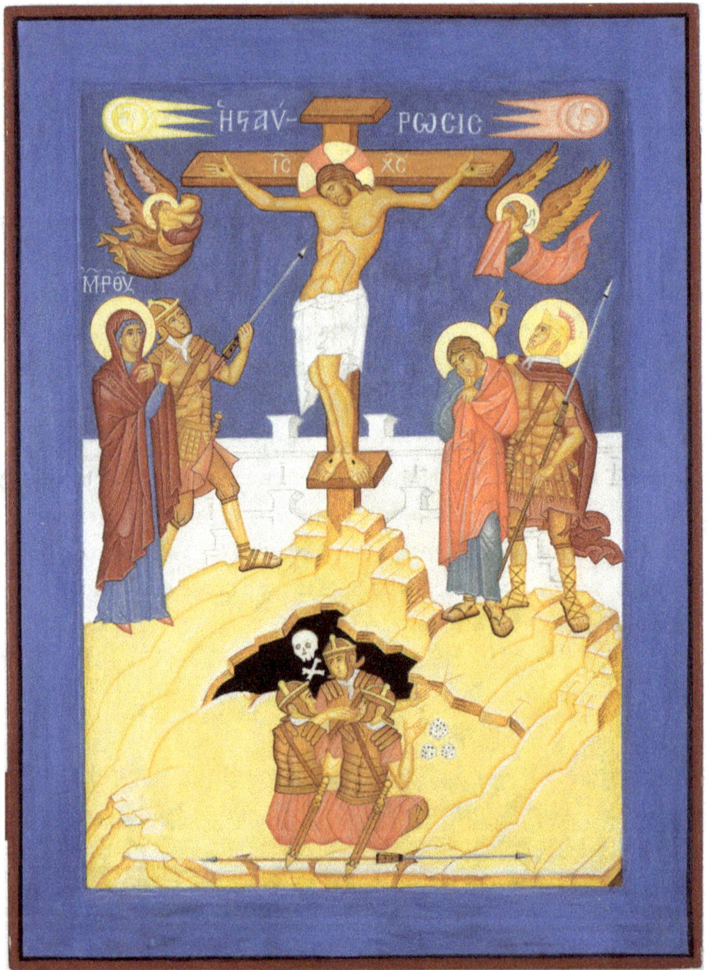

Readings for reflection:

Mark 15:20–47; Matthew 27:31–66; Luke 23:32–56; John 19:16–42

There can be no convincing argument that, in historical terms, the crucifixion of Jesus was anything other than a cruel judicial murder, perpetrated by the blind bureaucratic mechanism of a viciously oppressive empire.

Jesus' death was, in the eyes of the imperial power governing what was considered a remote and troublesome outpost, just one more punishment meted out to just one more local miscreant. Crucifixion was an almost daily occurrence and a common sight throughout the "civilized" Roman world. Death on a cross was a punishment for non-Roman citizens, low-bred malefactors, and slaves. As an apparatus of "justice," its aim was to dehumanize the person convicted, denuding him literally of all dignity and value as a person. Here was the brute force of Rome in operation, crushing all opposition and rebellion against the dominant social order.

When Christians, therefore, took up the cross as the symbol of their movement (which they did long before the age of Constantine) and proclaimed a crucified "criminal"—a "dehumanized" backwater "nobody"—as their "Lord and God," it was quite consciously and intentionally a slap against the might of the empire—indeed, against the "world" or "cosmos" itself. Without irony, they held up this bloody, damned symbol of Roman shaming as a sign of *their* victory over the worst the world could throw at them. They were rejecting Roman intimidation by their defiant choice of identification.

In the fourth century, Ephrem of Syria (306–373), one of the greatest of the Syriac fathers, could speak of the cross in such unabashedly triumphal terms as this: "Death had its own way when our Lord went out from Jerusalem carrying his cross; but when by a loud cry from that cross he summoned the dead from the underworld, death was powerless to prevent it . . . We give glory to you, Lord, who raised up your cross to span the jaws of death like a bridge by which souls might pass from the region of the dead to the land of the living."[6] We might regard this extolling of the cross as being more suited to the resurrection of Christ, and indeed it seems to mirror in words the icon which illustrates the next mystery. But Ephrem sees in the cross and the crucifixion of Jesus not just a willing sacrifice for sin and a succumbing to death, but the defeat of death's power over humankind itself and, in fact, the whole of creation. In treating the crucifixion of Jesus in terms of cosmic victory rather than as a single man's horrific suffering and death, Ephrem was a typical representative of Eastern Christian faith (even if he was also outstanding in his talent for the lyrical articulation of it). We find the language of acclamation and exultation again and again in the writings of the early church when they deal with the cross of Christ.

6. Ephrem, *Sermon on our Lord*, 3–4, 9. Reading for Friday of the third week of Easter; Wright, *Readings for the Daily Office*, 197.

When we arrive at this mystery, we are finally at the core of the Christian faith. Much ink has been spilled about Jesus' crucifixion and what it means for believers, beginning with the apostolic writings. A variety of "theories" regarding Jesus' death and how it brought about "atonement" (at-one-ment = reconciliation) with God have been devised over the millennia to explain the mystery, and these are (regardless of each theory's distinctive focus) central to every systematic and dogmatic theology. Faith in the sacrificial nature of Jesus' death is the essential matter of each theory. The crucifixion of Jesus, Christians believe, bestowed forgiveness and took away "the sin of the world." So it was that Paul could write to the Corinthians that "for our sake [God] made [Christ] to be sin [or, a sin offering] who knew no sin, so that in him we might become the righteousness of God" (2 Cor 5:21).

For the ancient church and for the Christian East still, the most astounding aspect of the cross is that it was there that God, whose timeless nature is incapable of dying, met death in time and space. The drama as played out is this: Death tries to "swallow up" Jesus, not knowing that God's immortal nature is "hidden" in Christ, whose mortal human nature is the "bait." This mythological language is common in the Eastern patristic tradition and numerous citations could be garnered to make the point. In Christ, the eternal source of all life and creation entered, so to speak, into the "belly" of death and—because it was indestructible—destroyed death from within. Death or Hades is often personified in Christian art as having the head of a gigantic monster with distended jaws, into which souls are fed or out of which they are freed by the risen Lord, depending on the subject of the depiction.

In classical Christian thought, no representation in word or art of the crucifixion was ever considered complete without reference to the resurrection, and likewise no representation in word or art of the resurrection was ever considered complete without the "victorious" cross in view. Together the cross and resurrection constituted a single, indissoluble work of God, and that work was the overcoming of death's grip on creation. That victory, set in motion by Christ, may not yet be fully realized on the cosmic scale, but it was the catalyst and assurance of universal restoration in the future age. This is why Paul could pronounce with such confidence that, when chronological time reaches its eternal goal, "the last enemy to be destroyed is death" (1 Cor 15:26). To put it succinctly, in ancient and Eastern Christianity, Jesus' death and resurrection is inclusive of everyone and everything: "'I, when I am lifted up from the earth, will draw *all* to myself.' He said this to show by what death [i.e., suspended on the cross] he was to die" (John 12:32–33; emphasis added and translation amended). Or, as Paul put it, "God was in Christ, reconciling the world unto himself" (2 Cor 5:19 KJV).

In one sense, of course, God can be said to be involved in every death. Biologically speaking, death is an aspect of life on earth and always has been. Theologically speaking, however, created life "lives, moves, and has its being in God," and not even a sparrow falls to the earth "without the Father's will" (see Acts 17:28 and Matt 10:29). Death, then, cannot be said to occur "outside" of God, who is omnipresent.

But, in another sense, God is "revealed" to each sentient creature according to its capacity to "know" God. In Jesus, God is made knowable to the human creation. God can be said to be known in many ways to human beings—through creation in all its incomprehensible diversity (see Rom 1:19–20), through the wisdom revealed in every culture, through meditation and prayer, and so on. But, in Christ, the "Word" or "Reason" of God took on human nature and revealed the divine in a way that human beings could recognize. Jesus is "God with us," "Emmanuel" (Matt 1:23), and he is "with us" not only in living an exemplary life and giving us exemplary instruction, but by even dying a death like ours. And, in fact, he died a cruel death inflicted by human hands and commensurate with the worst death one can die. He becomes, furthermore, identified on the cross with human sin itself, so much so that he can cry out, in the opening words of Psalm 22, "My God, my God, why hast thou forsaken me?" (Mark 15:34; Matt 27:46; it is to be noted that Psalm 22 ends on a note of victory, not despair). And in his death, he "takes away the sin of the world" (John 1:29). What Christ reveals, so Christians believe, is that God is present in our dying and even in our sin ("sin" means "to go off-course"): the first he overcomes by entering into it and overcoming it, the latter he defeats through forgiveness and—ultimately and with our cooperation—purgation of its effects.

All of that might be a lot to take on board, but it is essentially a message of hope and encouragement. The meaning of the cross for us is multilayered. We are to understand that death is not the last word, but life beyond death is; that hopelessness is not endless, however bleak our very existence may appear to us in our worst circumstances; and that our consciences, darkened by sins and failures, even those which seem to be beyond the possibility of forgiveness, have the prospect of final purification. The cross of Christ signifies all that for those who walk the Christian path. And it is a message that embraces in its universality the whole human race.

Our icon has one feature in it that points to this last aspect in a striking way. We see Jesus crucified between heaven and earth, the sun and moon's presence suggesting the involvement of the entire cosmos, and the two angels—covering their faces in mourning, amazement, and horror—indicating that the celestial orders behold the unfolding of this astounding drama. At the foot of the cross, following the account in John's Gospel, stand the mother of Jesus and the beloved disciple (Mary and John). Two soldiers roll dice for his garment at the base of the mount. Flanking the cross are two more soldiers standing. One points heavenward, suggesting that he is astonished by something in the heavens (the coming darkness?). The other is grasping his lance after piercing the side of Christ—we can see that Jesus' side is already wounded. And then there is that feature I mentioned above when discussing the icon of the Nativity, the one that suggests the universality of the effects of Jesus' death. In fact, this feature—which is common to icons depicting the crucifixion in the East—has a corresponding feature in the Resurrection icon that immediately follows this one, as we will see. But here we see, in a cave-like space directly below the cross, a skull and two crossed bones.

The first thing we note about this feature is that this skull reminds us that "Golgotha" means "the place of the skull." In tradition, though, this came to mean that this was the place where Adam, the first human being, was buried. Adam (the name means something like "earthling") is a "corporate person"—in other words, as the first human he contains *all* humanity in himself. Adam and Eve *are* the human race *in its entirety*. Jesus is "the last Adam," the one who takes to himself human nature and becomes the new beginning for the race (see 1 Cor 15:42–50). His death is united to our death, which is why it is Adam's skull that lies directly beneath his feet as he dies. Adam's skull is the symbol both of Adam's death and ours—it is, in a sense, all our graves that lie below Jesus' cross. His coming resurrection, which will be the subject of the next mystery and icon, will likewise involve Adam and, by implication, all humanity. And there, again, we will see both Adam and Eve (and, in them, ourselves) together resurrected with Jesus.

Keep that in mind as we turn to our next mystery and keep in mind, too, those words of Ephrem we have already cited above: "We give glory to you, Lord, who raised up your cross to span the jaws of death like a bridge by which souls might pass from the region of the dead to the land of the living."

Fourth Set: The "Glorious" Mysteries

Regeneration

The Sixteenth Mystery

The Resurrection of Christ

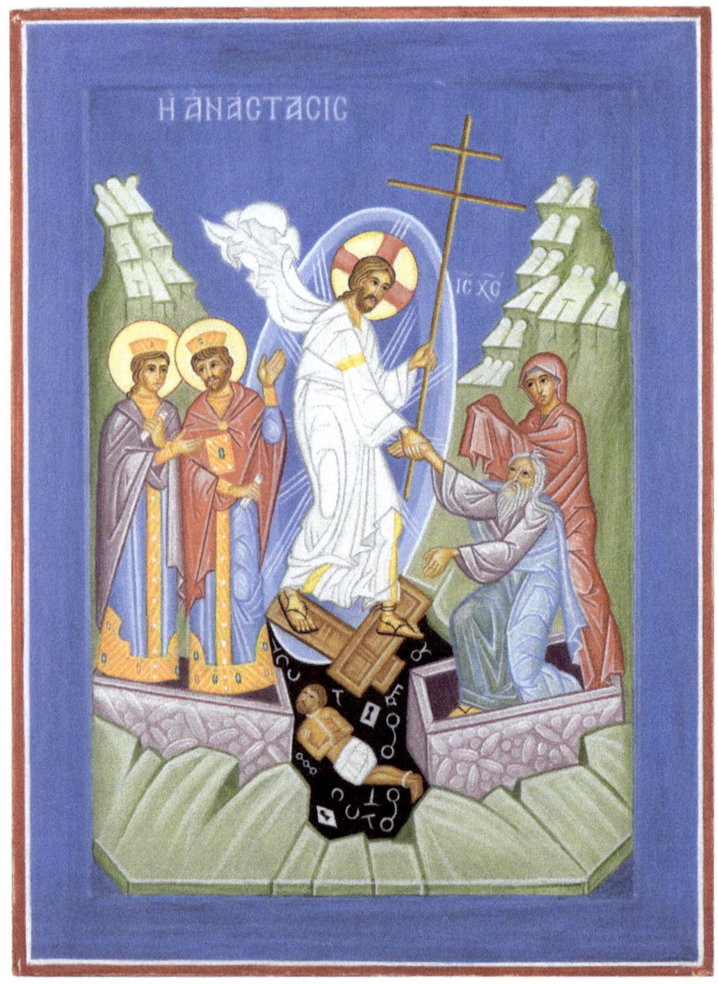

Readings for reflection:

> Mark 16:1–18; Matthew 28:1–20; Luke 24:1–49; John 20:1–21:25; Colossians 3:1–3

For the early Christians, the good news about Jesus was the proclamation of victory accomplished. With Christ had come reconciliation with God, and the gospel was the joyful announcement of this *fait accompli*. The "great commission" that Jesus gave to his followers, according to Matthew's Gospel (28:18–20), was that they should go into the world with the message and gather together all who heard and believed, making them disciples of "the Way." In the Letter to the Ephesians, we find one of a number of encapsulations of that message in the New Testament; its vision is universal in scope, and it expresses what the resurrection and ascension of Christ signified to the earliest believers: "God, who is rich in mercy, out of the great love with which he loved us, even *when we were dead* through our trespasses, made us *alive together with Christ* (by grace you have been saved), and *raised us up with him*, and made us sit with him in the heavenly places in Christ Jesus, that in the coming ages he might show the immeasurable riches of his grace in kindness toward us in Christ Jesus" (Eph 2:4–7; emphasis added). Note in this passage who they were who are described as having been "dead"—"we" were. Then note who they were who were "made alive" in union with Christ in his resurrection—again, "we" were. And, lastly, note who are even now (spiritually speaking) ascended with him into "the heavenly places"—and, again, it is "we" who are. What is to be noted is that the resurrection/ascension, in the belief of the early Christians, was an inclusive, corporate event.

The gospel of the early church was that the resurrection and ascension of Christ included (at least, potentially) all humanity. They were not simply the consummate acts of a single individual. For one thing, the ancient world knew nothing of the concept of individualism as it has developed and become widespread throughout modern Western culture. Christ was viewed from the beginning by the church as a "corporate person"—indeed, as "the last Adam." Just as "the first Adam" was understood to have contained within himself the entirety of the human race, so Christ contained within himself the same. It was considered a given that the human race is one in essence, divided into families and tribes and nations, but still one. The individual had value as a microcosm of the whole. The ancients, we might say, knew something foundational and irrefutable, but which we have largely forgotten: they knew that everyone is connected to everyone else who has ever lived. Nothing we do is ever done solely on an individual basis. It always involves others in one way or another. Independence is an illusion and radical individualism has never existed and can never exist.

It was this understanding of corporate humanity and the corresponding corporate personhood of Christ, of which baptism was the sacramental expression (see Rom 6:3-5), that underlay Paul's frequent reference to the baptized as those who are "in Christ." For Paul, it was not so much the case that "original" or "ancestral" sin (which is variously explained in different ecclesiastical traditions, but essentially means that the whole human race, whatever its many strengths, has a deeply ingrained tendency to do wrong) is "in us." Rather, Paul might have argued that we are "in it," because we are corporately "in Adam." The "fall" (an unfortunate term) was no more a datable past event than the first few chapters of Genesis are simple historiography. "Adam and Eve" are the entire human race in microcosm, and the "fall" is a perennial event, both corporate and personal in nature. For us, then, to be "in Adam" means that we share a common human reality. We are called to reflect "God's image," but we are also plagued by confused motives and bestial passions (Mark 7:14–23; Rom 7:21–24) and faced finally with the fear of death (e.g., Rom 5:12). Being "in Adam" means that we are as a species caught up in a network across time of mortality and failure. As Paul put it, "all have sinned and fall short" of our destined goal, which was and is to share in "the glory of God" (Rom 3:23). It is within this conceptual context that Paul refers to Christ as "the last Adam" (1 Cor 15:42–50). In other words, Christ is the new point of ultimate reference for the human race and the one who brings it to its final completion. In Paul's words, "as in Adam all die, so also in Christ shall all be made alive" (1 Cor 15:22). Note, again, the corporate nature of that statement: *all* die in Adam and *all* are made alive in Christ.

It is this same conviction that we find inferred in a few somewhat difficult (and sometimes downplayed) passages in the canonical New Testament.[1] One such passage is Matthew's description of the cataclysmic events that transpired following Jesus' death, especially this bit: "the earth shook, and the rocks were split; the tombs also were opened, and many bodies of the saints who had fallen asleep were raised, and coming out of the tombs after his resurrection they went into the holy city and appeared to many" (Matt 27:51b–53). There is some confusion here in Matthew's chronology—apparently, the earthquake shook open these saints' tombs at Jesus' death, and their bodies were raised, and yet he says that they did not go into the holy city until after Jesus had first risen. Whatever explanation one might venture for Matthew's elaboration on the crucifixion/resurrection

1. A beautifully illustrated, informative, and enjoyable look at this subject, with emphasis on the iconography of the resurrection of Christ, is John Dominic Crossan and Sarah Sexton Crossan's *Resurrecting Easter*. Chapter 4 ("He Did Not Rise Alone"), 61–73, is of particular interest here.

story, one thing is certain: Matthew's Gospel assumes that Jesus' resurrection was not simply an individual affair. It included others.

The tradition that Jesus had descended, upon his death, to the mythological realm of the dead (Hades) and proclaimed there the good news, is an early one—so early, in fact, that we find it alluded to also in the New Testament, in two obscure passages in the First Letter of Peter. There we read that Christ preached to the recalcitrant ancients of Noah's time: "For Christ also died for sins once for all, the righteous for the unrighteous, that he might bring us to God, being put to death in the flesh but made alive in the spirit; in which [presumably, before his resurrection] he went and preached to the spirits in prison, who formerly did not obey, when God's patience waited in the days of Noah" (1 Pet 3:18–20a). This scenario is brought up again just a handful of verses later: "For this is why the gospel was preached even to the dead, that though judged in the flesh like men, they might live in the spirit like [or "according to"] God" (1 Pet 4:6). We can only speculate what the text means by "the dead . . . liv[ing] in the spirit like God," but the gist of both these statements from 1 Peter, taken together, is clear enough: the spirits of the dead heard the gospel and were thereby rescued from "prison" and given the opportunity to be transformed by the power of Christ. Again, Jesus' death/resurrection is said to have enfolded others in its embrace.

The emptying of Hades of its "prisoners" is elaborated in later literary and iconographic depictions (including our icon) of Christ's resurrection—for the overcoming of death's power over the human race is the essential meaning of Jesus' "resurrection." The famous Easter homily of John Chrysostom (c. 347–407) expresses this in majestically poetical terms:

> Let none lament their poverty, for the Universal Kingdom has been revealed.
>
> Let none mourn their transgressions, for Pardon has dawned from the tomb!
>
> Let no one fear Death, for the Savior's death has set us free!
>
> He that was taken by Death has annihilated it!
>
> He descended into Hell [Hades], and took Hell [Hades] captive!
>
> He embittered it when it tasted of His Flesh! And anticipating this Isaiah exclaimed, "Hell [Hades] was embittered when it encountered thee in the lower regions." It was embittered, for it was

> abolished! It was embittered, for it was mocked! It was embittered, for it was purged! It was embittered, for it was despoiled [of its captives]! It was embittered, for it was bound in chains![2]

> It took a body, and face to face met God! It took earth, and encountered Heaven! It took what it saw [the human nature of Christ], but crumbled before what it had not seen [the divine nature of Christ]![3]

Apocryphal literature carried on this homiletic and catechetical tradition in elaborate and dramatic style. For example, in *The Gospel of Nicodemus* (late seventh century), Christ descends to the underworld to rescue all the imprisoned dead, chief among whom is the representative of the whole human race, Adam: "[T]he King of Glory stretched out his right hand, and took hold of our forefather Adam and raised him up. Then turning also to the rest [of the dead], he said: 'Come with me, all you who have suffered death through the tree which this man touched; for, behold, I again raise you all up through the tree of the Cross' . . . And setting out to paradise, he took hold of our forefather Adam by the hand, and delivered him, and all the just, to the archangel Michael."[4] And earlier in the same work, these words are placed in the mouth of Joseph of Arimathea, indicating again the corporate nature of the resurrection and referring back to the text in Matthew cited above (27:51b–53) and to the "saints" who had risen from their tombs to "appear to many": "Joseph says: 'And why do you wonder that Jesus has risen? *But it is wonderful that he has not risen alone*, but that he has also raised many others of the dead, who have appeared in Jerusalem to many" (emphasis added).[5]

Another ancient homily, attributed to the fourth-century apologist Epiphanius, but actually written pseudonymously in the seventh century, put the same mythological scene in the form of a powerful and moving monologue spoken by Christ to Adam, in the underworld:

> I order you, O sleeper, to awake. I did not create you to be held a prisoner in Hades. Rise from the dead, for I am the life of the dead. Rise up, work of my hands, you who were created in my image.

2. Note the bound figure in our icon, in the abyss beneath the fallen doors and the feet of Christ, surrounded by the locks and bolts that formerly secured the captive dead. That is the personification of Hades.

3. Wright, *Readings for the Daily Office*, 175.

4. *The Gospel of Nicodemus*, ch. 8 (24), 437.

5. *The Gospel of Nicodemus*, ch. 1 (17), 435.

> Rise, let us leave this place, for you are in me, and I in you; *together we form only one person and we cannot be separated . . .*
>
> I slept on the cross and a sword pierced my side for you who slept in Paradise and brought forth Eve from your side. My side has healed the pain in yours. My sleep will rouse your sleep in Hades. The sword that pierced me has sheathed the sword that was turned against you.
>
> Rise, let us leave this place. The Enemy led you out of the earthly Paradise. I will not restore you to that Paradise, but I will enthrone you in Heaven. I forbade you the tree that was only a symbol of life, but see, *I who am life itself am now one with you.* I appointed cherubim to guard you as slaves are guarded, but now I make them worship you as God. The throne formed by cherubim awaits you, its bearers swift and eager. The bridal chamber is adorned, the banquet is ready, the eternal dwelling places are prepared, the treasure houses of all good things lie open. The Kingdom of Heaven has been prepared for you from all eternity.[6]

It is this consciously mythological depiction that carries over into the Eastern church's traditional iconography of Jesus' resurrection, as our icon shows. Christian art in both East and West, of course, also depict Jesus alone emerging from the tomb. The latter is not a symbolic representation of a corporate resurrection, needless to say, but of the resurrection event itself (it is worth noting that the canonical Gospels themselves never attempt a description of Jesus' resurrection). Whereas the motif of Jesus rising alone from the tomb was to become the standard depiction of Jesus' resurrection in the West, it is rather the mythological defeat of Hades and the releasing of its prisoners that, over time, became the definitive motif in the East.

The iconography of the corporate resurrection often shows an array of biblical figures freshly raised from the bonds of death—Abel, patriarchs, prophets, John the Baptist, and so on. In our icon, the number has been reduced to just four rescued figures, Adam and Eve to the viewer's right and King David and King Solomon to the viewer's left. David and Solomon (the latter young and beardless) together indicate Jesus' Davidic lineage. Even more to the point, a handful of David's psalms were understood to prophesy Jesus' resurrection and his rescue of those in bondage.[7] Likewise, the pseudepigraphical *Odes of Solomon* (probably originally written in

6. *Liturgy of the Hours*, 497–98. Emphasis added.

7. See, for example, Pss 16:10; 23:4; 40:2; 49:15; 71:20; 86:13; 130:1; 139:11–12.

Aramaic/Syriac) may be the earliest texts outside the New Testament that speak of Christ's descent to the underworld, and perhaps this association further explains Solomon's presence in the iconographic motif.[8] Next to Christ himself, Adam and Eve are the most important figures in the icon. Jesus grasps the limp arm of Adam and pulls him from his tomb, with Eve directly behind him. Whereas in the crucifixion icon we saw the skull and bones of the dead and buried Adam, here we see the patriarch of the human race, along with the race's matriarch, forcefully pulled by Christ into resurrection life. The doors of the underworld have been flattened and lie over the abyss in the form of the cross; and cast into that abyss, along with all his bolts, locks, and chains of imprisonment, is the bound and chained personification of Hades and death itself—defeated and consigned by Christ the victor to oblivion. The entire motif is dynamic, and its meaning is clear: Jesus' resurrection was not merely an event of his rising from death alone, but with him—and "in him"—the human race was raised and given the promise of everlasting life.

The mythological scene was, of course, never meant to be taken literally. "Hades" personified was a metaphor for death. After all, how can something simultaneously so mysterious and so mundane as death be depicted at all? The "conquering" of death was inferred from the good news of Jesus' resurrection—the one who had died so appallingly was no longer in the tomb but had shown himself to his followers. And the interpretation of how his resurrection effects the whole of humankind (and even the whole cosmos) was the fruit of those followers struggling to come to terms with who Jesus was. What was clearly understood by the earliest believers was that something astounding had been revealed in and by Jesus, and that his death and resurrection were not simply *doctrine*, but realities in

8. Most notably, *Odes of Solomon* 17 and 42. The especially relevant verses are:

"And from there he gave me the way of his paths, and I opened the doors which were closed. And I shattered the bars of iron, for my own iron(s) had grown hot and melted before me. And nothing appeared closed to me, because I was the opening of everything. And I went toward all my bondsmen in order to loose them; that I might not abandon anyone bound or binding . . . and they received my blessing and lived, and they were gathered to me and were saved." (17:9–12, 15)

"Sheol saw me and was shattered, and Death ejected me and many with me. I have been vinegar and bitterness to it, and I went down with it as far as its depths . . . And I made a congregation of living among his dead; and I spoke with them by living lips; in order that my word may not fail. And those who had died ran toward me; and they cried out and said, 'Son of God, have pity on us. And deal with us according to your kindness and bring us out from the chains of darkness.'" (42:11–12, 14–16)

See Charlesworth, *Old Testament Pseudepigrapha, Volume 2*, 750–51, 771.

which we participate—in which humanity participates. In Christ had been established an indissoluble at-one-ment between humanity and the divine. But the best "proof" or "evidence" of the resurrection was something that happened *within believers*. Somehow, through their corporate and personal encounter with Christ's Spirit, they knew themselves to be "in Christ" and already "risen with him"—not something that was future-tense in perspective only, but also present-tense. One can only suppose that this was a *realization*—mystical, contemplative, and brought home to believers through liturgy and deep meditation (see Matt 6:6; John 14:23).

I conclude here with verses that will reappear in the next reflection, which will be about Christ's ascension: "If then you have been raised with Christ, seek the things that are above, where Christ is, seated at the right hand of God. Set your minds on things that are above, not on things that are on earth. For you have died, and your life is hid with Christ in God" (Col 3:1–3). Here I will focus only on two lines, not even full sentences.

First, "for you have died." The Christian contemplative tradition begins with this realization. "In Christ" Christians are already "dead"—they died with Jesus in his crucifixion mystically, which is sacramentalized by baptism (see Rom 6:1–14). In other words, for those "in Christ" death is past and nothing—ultimately—to fear (even if the natural human reaction is to fear the process of *dying*). Or, put differently, Christians believe that they are "born anew," that they are resurrected. Which is why, second, the verses cited above from Colossians begin with the words, "If then you have been raised with Christ . . ." Through the mythological scenario it depicts, what our icon signifies is that the human family *has been* raised with Christ. In grasping the hand of "the first Adam," Jesus "the last Adam" is taking hold of all human beings and including them in his new life. That is the freeing truth that all are invited to contemplate inwardly ("set your minds on") and take to heart.

The Seventeenth Mystery

The Ascension of Christ

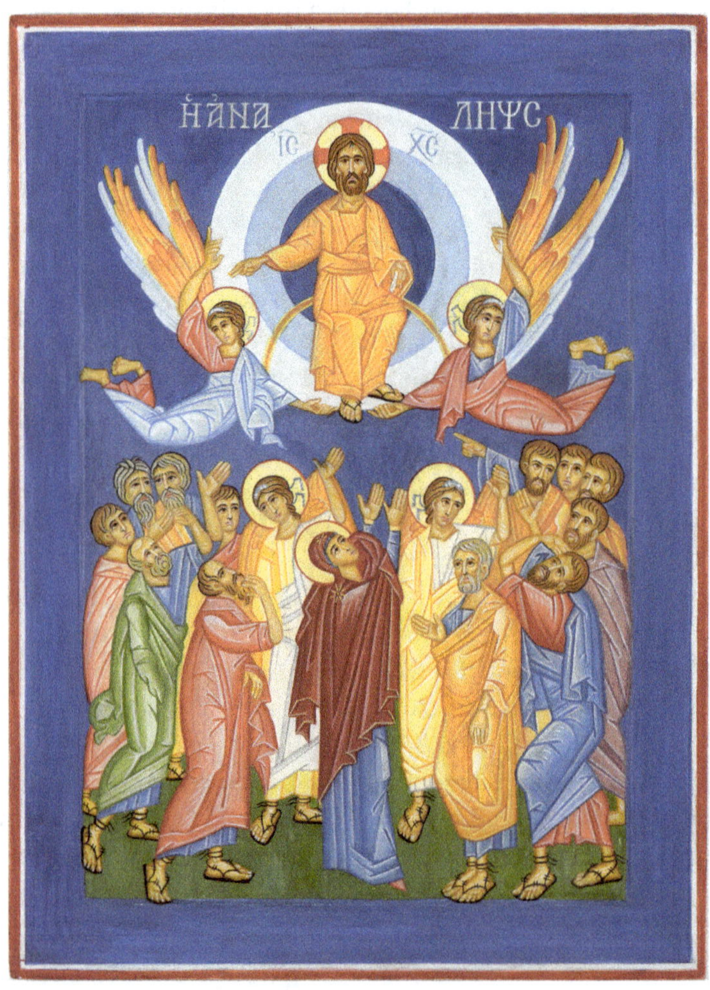

Readings for reflection:

> Luke 24:50–53; Acts 1:1–11; John 20:17; Romans 8:31–39; Ephesians 1:18–23; 4:10; Colossians 3:1–3

Only in the writings attributed to Luke—both in the Gospel and again in the book of Acts—is there a description of the ascension (or "taking up") of Jesus. It takes place outside Jerusalem, "as far as Bethany" (Luke 24:50), and the disciples are told to remain in Jerusalem until they receive from "on high" the "power" of the Holy Spirit (Luke 24:49; Acts 1:8). The other three Gospels do not tell about the ascension (unless one includes the later "longer ending" that was tacked on to the tail of Mark's).

Mark ends on an uncertain note. In the Greek text, it appears even to end mid-sentence. As has long been postulated, that Gospel may have lost both its original ending and beginning, which would explain the narrative's abrupt opening (with Jesus' baptism) and its ambiguous conclusion, which describes the frightened women fleeing the empty tomb and saying nothing about it. Although some scholars argue against that view, it seems more likely that Mark is missing its first and final portions. So, we do not know whether or not Mark had once included an ascension account. The Gospel as we have it leaves us hanging. Not so the other writings in the tradition.

Although neither the Gospel of Matthew nor the Gospel of John include an ascension account, both leave their readers with a word of assurance. Matthew, quite pointedly and in keeping with one of the themes of that particular Gospel, ends with Jesus' words to his disciples, assuring them of his continuing *presence* among them: "I am with you always, to the close of the age" (Matt 28:20). (It is also worth noting that Jesus meets with the eleven on a mountain in Galilee, not near Jerusalem as in the Lucan texts.) One of the themes running through Matthew is that Jesus is the promised "God with us" ("Emmanuel") of Isaiah 7:14. So it is that, when the church conducts its affairs after his resurrection, Jesus will still be with them: "For where two or three are gathered in my name, there am I in the midst of them" (Matt 18:20). The conclusion of Matthew, then, brings this theme to its completion: Christ will be among them until the end of time. Matthew leaves his church with a message of reassurance.

In John's Gospel, Jesus makes it clear to his disciples in the conventionally called "farewell discourse" and "high priestly prayer" (chapters 14–17) that he will depart and in his stead send them "another paraclete" to abide with them (identified as the Spirit of the Father; 14:16; 15:26). He tells them that he leaves and "will prepare a place for [them]" and "will come again and will take [them] to [himself]" (John 14:2–3). Nonetheless, John does not describe Jesus' departure. After his resurrection, Jesus tells Mary the Magdalene that she must not hold him, for he has "not yet ascended to the Father; rather, he says to her, "go to my brethren and say to them, I am ascending to my Father and your Father, to my God and your God" (John

20:17). What this verse suggests is that, according to John, Jesus ascended after sending her off to his disciples and only after his ascension (occurring on the day of his resurrection) did he then appear to them. John's Gospel regards the ascension as the crowning moment of the resurrection, but it presents us with no account of that ascension. In the Johannine tradition, Jesus' ascension to the Father was the completing of his "glorification," for which Jesus had prayed before his arrest: "Father, glorify thou me in thy own presence with the glory which I had with thee before the world was made" (John 17:5). In summary, John's Gospel tells the good news that the Word descended from "glory" and gathered to himself "all" (John 12:32), and—having taken away "the sin of the cosmos"—was once again restored to his former "glory," after imparting to them the Holy Spirit—the "Paraclete"—to guide and encourage them in the interim. Again, as with Matthew's conclusion, John ends on a reassuring note.

The epistolary writings in the New Testament, as well as other early Christian literature, show how intense was the church's faith that Christ was living and sharing fully in the Father's glory and power, and that—in the Spirit, not "in the flesh"—he was fully present with them still. The authors of these writings describe his ascended, transcendent state with various metaphors drawn from the cultural and religious context they knew. So it is that, although Jesus during his earthly life had eschewed worldly power and (as a faithful Jew) certainly never assumed any cultic authority, he was accorded the esteemed titles of Lord, high priest, and heavenly advocate ("paraclete") by the early believers, even though at the same time the developing churches also shied away from using cultic titles for their ministers during the first two centuries.

In Paul's writings, Jesus is said to be "at the right hand of God," an image we find in Psalm 110:1 and that indicates a share in another's authority, and that he must "reign until he has put all his enemies under his feet" (Rom 8:34; 1 Cor 15:25)—and "the last enemy to be destroyed is death" (1 Cor 15:26). Jesus is, in other words, the Messianic king, now reigning over the cosmos until all that must be fulfilled is indeed fulfilled.

In the Letter to the Hebrews, Jesus is the "great high priest who has passed through the heavens," "designated by God . . . after the order of Melchizedek," "who is seated at the right hand of the throne of the Majesty in heaven, a minister in the sanctuary and the true tent which is set up not by man but by the Lord" (Heb 4:14; 5:10; 8:1–2). He is, in contrast to those serving in the earthly Temple in Jerusalem, which is only a copy and shadow of the heavenly and true sanctuary invisible to human eyes (Heb 8:5), the "real thing." The epistle encourages its readers to take to heart the faith that Christ is in the heavens on their behalf: "Since then we have a great high priest who has passed through the heavens, Jesus, the Son of God, let us hold fast our confession. For we have not a high priest who is unable to sympathize with our weaknesses, but one who in every respect has been tempted [better: "tested" or "proved"] as we are, yet without sin. Let us then with confidence draw near to the throne of grace, that we may receive mercy and find grace to help in time of need" (Heb 4:14–16).[9]

In the First Letter of John, Christ is the "advocate with the Father" (1 John 2:1). The word *advocate* or *paraclete* literally means one who "comes alongside," who encourages and strengthens. The assurance in John's letter is that sin need not be the last word for the believer who stumbles and falls. "If we confess our sins," writes the author of the epistle, "he is faithful and just, and will forgive our sins, and cleanse us from all unrighteousness" (1 John 1:9). "My little children," he continues, "I am writing this to you so that you may not sin; but if any one does sin, we have an advocate with the Father, Jesus Christ the righteous; and he is the expiation for our sins, and not for ours only but also for the sins of the whole world" (1 John 2:1–2). There is in 1 John, as in Hebrews, the image of sacrifice and priesthood. Christ the paraclete has offered himself as an expiation for sins, and his "blood . . . cleanses us from all sin" (1 John 1:7). Again, we have a word of encouragement and consolation, and it is based on the faith that Jesus' presence "in heaven" with the Father is for the sake of his people and also that of "the whole world."

It should be obvious even to the casual reader that the messages of encouragement we find in these texts are not stoical exhortations for believers

9. It is important to note that this writing was probably addressed to Jewish Christians undergoing specific trials—physical persecution, perhaps, but even more likely exclusion from the synagogues, though it is impossible to be certain of the context. We can be fairly certain, though, that when the text says that Jesus was "in every respect . . . tested as we are, yet without sin," the phrase "in every respect" does not mean that he was tempted to "sin" in every imaginable way. Not only would such a reading be completely out of context, but also patently absurd. The text means, quite specifically, that his trust in God—his "confession" of faith—was "tested" to the very limit—as theirs is—by suffering (Heb 5:7–10), and yet he held fast to his confession. Likewise, in their own similar temptations to "give up," they must prove themselves by "holding fast." The "sin" referred to in verse 16 is the "sin" of not holding on to their confession. To help them in their weakness, though, is the great high priest who has sympathy for them and gives them, when floundering and weak, access to mercy and the "throne of grace." Therefore, they should have confidence and not despair.

to keep stiff upper lips in the face of Christ's *absence* from his people. On the contrary, they attest to the early believers' conviction that Christ was still *present* and abiding among them. There is no ultimate conflict, then, between the ascension narratives of Luke and the ascension-less conclusion of Matthew. The early Christian communities believed that the "taking up" of Jesus to God, in fact, was the guarantee that his continuing presence extended throughout the cosmos, no less than in their gatherings. When God "raised him from the dead and made him sit at his right hand in the heavenly places," his "fullness" was not said to be confined to "the church, which is his body," but also to fill "all in all" or "everything"—"He who descended is he who also ascended far above the heavens, that he might fill all things" (Eph 1:20, 22–23; 4:10). So it was that Paul could make his bold assertion that, in effect, there was no escaping the all-embracing presence of the risen and "enthroned" Christ, which in turn means that there is no eluding the universal love of God manifested in him: "Who shall separate us from the love of Christ? . . . For I am sure that neither death, nor life, nor angels, nor principalities, nor things present, nor things to come, nor powers, nor height, nor depth, nor anything else in all creation, will be able to separate us from the love of God in Christ Jesus our Lord" (Rom 8:35, 38–39).

Whatever the metaphor employed—enthroned king, high priest, advocate—it is safe to assume that early Christians understood that the reality to which these metaphors pointed was different and beyond any human power of expression. Earthly kings, priests, and advocates were only pale comparisons to the risen and exalted Christ, whose divine presence filled all things and whose love was inexhaustible. Whatever trials they encountered, whatever sins they stumbled into and repented of, whatever terrors the world threw at them, however long or short their lives might prove to be in this world, the early communities of believers were certain that Christ was with them. They experienced the truth of what Julian of Norwich would write many centuries later, in her typically consoling way, that she had heard directly from the living Christ: "It is true that sin is cause of all this pain, but all shall be well, and all shall be well, and all manner of thing shall be well."[10]

Our icon depicts the ascension in such a way that what is communicated to the viewer is Christ's continuing presence. Instead of a figure

10. Julian of Norwich, *Revelations of Divine Love*, ch. 27. An especially useful edition of Julian's great book, with ample notes, introductory material, and appendices, is John-Julian, *The Complete Julian of Norwich*. The pertinent quote is found there on p. 149.

in the act of rising or soaring aloft, we see him seated within a globe signifying both heaven and the cosmos. He is not going anywhere; he has arrived. He sits, in fact, enthroned above the arc of what appears to be a rainbow. The visual message is that he "fills" and guides all things. Two angels attend him in heaven and two more angels, as in the book of Acts, exhort the gathered apostles on earth. In the center of the ring of apostles stands the supplicating figure of Mary. Although she is not present in the Lucan accounts of the ascension, she is present here in her role as supreme symbol of the church. The Apostle Paul is also depicted as present, although this is clearly ahistorical (a reminder that icons are not "religious art," but "sacred art"—which is to say, symbolic in nature and not simply illustrative). One reason for his inclusion, apart from his rising prestige in the early centuries of the church, could be because Paul had much to say about Christ both as ascended and as present in the church's midst. The meaning of the icon, in accord with the New Testament and other writings of the early church, is that Christ is not absent from the church or the world. He and "the throne of grace" are approachable everywhere and always: "I am with you always, to the close of the age."

Finally, on a psychological and spiritual note, "ascension" or "ascent" is a hallmark of the Christian inner life. Returning to the same passage in Colossians that we looked at in our last mystery, we read again the exhortation to the epistle's readers: "If you have been raised with Christ, seek the things that are above, where Christ is, seated at the right hand of God. Set your minds on things that are above, not on things that are on earth" (Col 3:1–2). Clearly, this is not intended to be understood in any literal sense. Its meaning is self-evidently spiritual. Within our selves we are to "ascend" to "where Christ is." We might today say that we should practice a form of contemplative prayer or meditation that draws us into a "higher consciousness." Indeed, since we believe that Christ is everywhere present, as we have seen that the concept of his "ascension" indicates, then he is accessible within our selves, too. We can "rise" to him within our own "hearts." By silencing our mouths and—with practice—also our chattering minds, breathing with the Holy Spirit (literally, "holy breath"), and "abiding" in him (see, for example, John 14:23; 15:1–11), we will know what it is to share spiritually in Christ's ascension. The language of such spiritual ascent has long been central in the mystical language of the church, from the New Testament writings, to (for example) Gregory of Nyssa's *Life of Moses*, to the treatises that go under the name of Pseudo-Dionysius the

Areopagite, to John Climacus's *Ladder of Divine Ascent*, to Bernard's *On the Steps of Humility and Pride* and the stages of love in his *On Loving God*, to Bonaventure's *Journey of the Mind to God*, to the ascent of the mind above "the cloud of unknowing" in the great treatise of the same name, to John of the Cross's *Ascent of Mount Carmel* . . . and so on. The perennial invitation is that we "raise" our minds from the mundane to "the things that are above, where Christ is." If we make that our daily practice for however long we can manage to do it, we will come to understand more fruitfully what lies at the core of Jesus' ascension and what its message of his abiding *presence* means to us.

The Eighteenth Mystery

The Descent of the Spirit

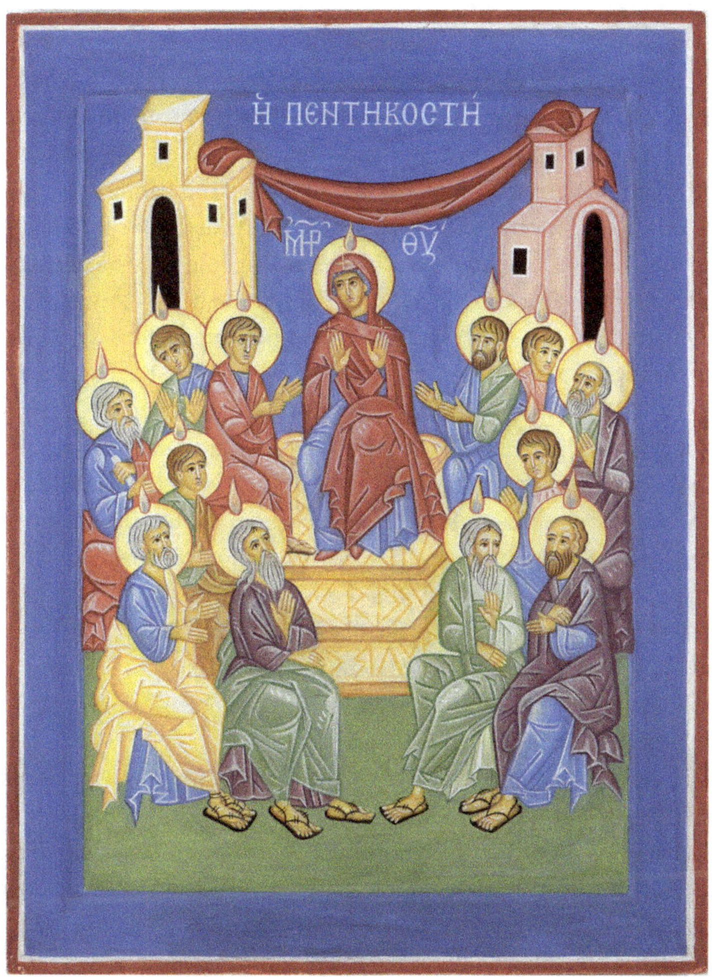

Readings for reflection:

> Acts 2:1–42; John 14:15–16, 25–26; 15:26; 16:7–11; 20:19–23; 2 Corinthians 3:17–18

When the early Christians claimed that the risen and ascended Christ "filled all things," was still present with them "until the end of the age," and was, with the Father, "abiding" with them and within their "hearts" (see Eph 4:10; Matt 28:20; John 14:23; Gal 4:6), they were affirming their belief in "the Spirit of the Son." And the Spirit of the Son, they also affirmed, was also the eternal Spirit of God.

The identification was so categorical that Paul could even write that "the Lord" (a title he most frequently used for Jesus Christ) *is* "the Spirit" (2 Cor 3:18), apparently without any fear of being misunderstood by his readers. In saying this, he was not confusing the person of Jesus with "the Spirit," as if they were indistinguishable, but he was indicating that "the Lord Spirit" was the means by which Jesus Christ continued to be present and active among believers. In Paul's teaching, Christ could only be encountered now through the Spirit and no longer "in the flesh." "[T]hough we have known Christ after the flesh," he wrote, "yet now henceforth know we him [in the flesh] no more" (2 Cor 5:16, KJV). Whenever Paul spoke of "the flesh" of Christ in his epistles, he was specifically referring to Christ in his pre-resurrection life. His post-resurrection life had become omnipresent and could now be perceived everywhere—even within the disciple's innermost being. Along these same lines, Jesus' enigmatic but reassuring words in John's Gospel somewhat parallel Paul's teaching: "Nevertheless I tell you the truth: *it is to your advantage* that I go away, for if I do not go away, the Counselor [Paraclete, Advocate, Encourager = Spirit] will not come to you; but if I go, I will send him to you" (John 16:7; emphasis added). For John as well as Paul, in the wake of the ascension it is the Spirit's work that is most essential in the life of the follower of Christ.

The word *spirit* means "wind" or "gust" (the same word, in essence, as "ghost") or "breath." The divine Spirit was understood to be God's living, inexhaustible, permeating breath and the source of all contingent life. For the ancient Hebrews, this was taken quite literally. The very air one breathed was directly given by God; he was everywhere present and the immediate cause of every creature's life-breath. We can see this assumption in such texts as Psalm 104:29–30, which speaks of creaturely life and death in terms of *breath*: "When thou hidest thy face, [all creatures] are dismayed; when thou takest away their breath, they die and return to their dust. When thou sendest forth thy Spirit [literally, breath], they are created; and thou renewest the face of the ground." Ecclesiastes 3:19–21 says something similar:

> For the fate of the sons of men and the fate of beasts is the same; as one dies, so dies the other. They all have the same breath [or, spirit], and man has no advantage over the beasts; for all is vanity.

> All go to one place; all are from the dust, and all turn to dust again. Who knows whether the spirit [breath] of man goes upward and the spirit [breath] of the beast goes down to the earth?

And this from Ecclesiastes also: "[A]nd the dust returns to the earth as it was [when one dies], and the spirit [breath] returns to God who gave it" (Eccl 12:7).

Indeed, without God's "breath" operating upon the roiling chaos "in the beginning," there would have been no creation of any kind: "The earth was without form and void, and darkness was upon the face of the deep; and the Spirit [wind, breath] of God was moving over the face of the waters" (Gen 1:2). Nor would there have been the creation of man and woman without the breath/spirit of God: "[T]hen the LORD God formed man of dust from the ground, and breathed into his nostrils the breath of life; and man became a living being" (Gen 2:7). So it is that in describing the death of Jesus, Luke's account has him crying out from the cross in the words of Psalm 31:6: "Father, into thy hands I commit my spirit [breath]!" (Luke 23:46). And all four Gospels express his death in terms of Jesus either breathing his last or giving up his spirit/breath (Mark 15:37; Matt 27:50; Luke 23:46; John 19:30).

Death, in biblical idiom, is in fact always the exhalation of one's "last breath" and a "giving up of the spirit." This is because life itself was seen as a palpable, tangible participation in spirit. The distinction between such a palpable "natural" spirit/breath from God and God's "supernatural" power-bestowing Spirit/Breath has been sharply made by theologians down the ages—and even in the Scriptures, where many unresolved ambiguities are to be found, the two are often distinguished. For example, "the Spirit of the LORD" that strengthens Samson to slay the lion and tear binding ropes asunder (Judg 14:6; 15:14) is more than "natural" and certainly not his "life-breath"—it is a "supernatural" power that comes upon him. Admittedly, this particular example concerns a primitive idea of "Spirit." But in a much more sophisticated context than that of the book of Judges, the Spirit who speaks through the prophets of the Old Testament is regarded as an extraordinary gift of utterance and likewise not a "natural" gift.

Turning to the New Testament, the Spirit of God and Christ is also a "supernatural" gift of both power and utterance. He discloses "the mind of Christ," and in himself is both known and unknowable, a mystery hidden in the very intimacy of his indwelling presence. He abides among the members of Christ's body and is the church's deepest mystical reality, but—like the passing wind—he cannot be grasped or fully comprehended by the intellect: "The spirit/breath/wind blows where it wills, and you hear the sound of it, but you do not know whence it comes or whither it goes; so it is with every one who is born of the Spirit/breath/wind" (John 3:8; my rendering). And Paul puts it like this:

> But, as it is written, "What no eye has seen, nor ear heard, nor the heart of man conceived, what God has prepared for those who love him,"[11] God has revealed to us through the Spirit. For the Spirit searches everything, even the depths of God. For what person knows a man's thoughts except the spirit of the man which is in him? So also no one comprehends the thoughts of God except the Spirit of God . . . The spiritual man judges all things, but is himself to be judged by no one. "For who has known the mind of the Lord so as to instruct him?"[12] But we have the mind of Christ. (1 Cor 2:9–11, 15–16)

And it is the Spirit, not a sacred book (as important as that may be), around whom the disciples of Jesus are to be gathered: "When the Spirit of truth comes," Jesus says to his disciples in John's Gospel, "he will guide you into all the truth . . . He will glorify me, for he will take what is mine and declare it to you" (John 16:13–14). The Spirit takes precedence over the Scriptures because they can only be rightly interpreted "spiritually": "[F]or the scripture kills, but the Spirit gives life . . . but when a person turns to the Lord the veil [that obscures the spiritual meaning of scripture] is removed. Now the Lord is the Spirit . . ." (2 Cor 3:6, 16–17a, my rendering). We have, of course, seen ample evidence down the ages how the Scriptures can be mishandled and turned into instruments of abuse even by well-intentioned people.

Paul tells us why the Spirit must take priority over all else in the "spiritual" lives of Christ's followers, and this is the reason: It is only through the Spirit's hidden operation that Jesus' disciples can hope to be "transformed" into his image. The genuine goal for the believer in the Christian tradition means—as the Greek fathers in particular expressed it—"to become by grace what Christ is by nature." As Paul stated it, "But we all, with unveiled face beholding as in a glass [a metallic mirror] the glory of the Lord, are changed into the same image from glory to glory [that is, gradually], even as by the Spirit of the Lord" (2 Cor 3:18 KJV, altered slightly). The Spirit's invisible operations are made visible in the ongoing transformation of

11. See Isa 64:4.

12. Isa 40:13.

the disciple's character. Paul referred to this as the development of "the fruit"—the produce—"of the Spirit" in believers' lives: "But the fruit of the Spirit is love, joy, peace, patience, kindness, goodness, faithfulness, gentleness, self-control; against such there is no law" (Gal 5:22–23). Here, then, is the language of authentic Christian "spirituality"—the contemplation of Christ "in the Spirit" that finds its fruition in Christlike character. Anything less than this is a failure to understand what the gift of the Spirit means for the follower of Jesus.

We find two accounts in the New Testament of Jesus bestowing the Spirit on his followers, specifically as power for them to spread his message. In John's Gospel, Jesus appears to his disciples on the evening of the day of his resurrection. He breathes on them, telling them, "Receive the Holy Spirit. If you forgive the sins of any, they are forgiven; if you retain the sins of any, they are retained." His disciples are to be an extension of his ministry of forgiveness to those willing to receive it (see John 20:19–23). The second account of the Spirit's bestowal is much more dramatic in its details than John's. It is found in the second chapter of the book of Acts and it is this scene from Acts that, in stylized form, we see depicted in our icon.

The scene is Jerusalem, probably in the upper room mentioned in Acts 1:13 (or so we may presume, though it is not specifically designated; "the house" in 2:2 could possibly refer to a different location), where the nucleus of the first Christian community is gathered—the twelve apostles, possibly the 120 disciples mentioned in 1:15, including "the women and Mary the mother of Jesus, and [Jesus'] brothers" (Acts 1:14). It is the Jewish feast of Shavuot ("Weeks"; see Lev 23:15–21) or—as the Greek-speaking Jews called it—"Pentecost" ("Fiftieth"—celebrated fifty days after Passover). Suddenly there is the sound of "a mighty wind" and "tongues as of fire" rest upon all those present. Both wind and fire were customary symbols of the Spirit—of God's Breath (and breath brings with it the power of life itself). The disciples begin to speak in a variety of languages "as the Spirit gave them utterance" (Acts 2:4). The sound of the wind and the voices is tremendous enough to attract a crowd, a multitude of Jews from many nations who have gathered in Jerusalem for the feast. To this crowd Peter gives an address that "cuts" them "to the heart," and—so Acts tells us—"about three thousand souls" repented (had a change of heart), were baptized, and were added to the nascent community (Acts 2:41).

Our icon presents one version of this scene. The apostles are gathered around the central person of Mary, both because she is mentioned in

Acts 1:14, suggesting that she was present at the Pentecost event, and also because—as we saw in the Introduction—she was the premier symbol of the "virgin mother" church. Present, too, in the scene is the Apostle Paul—an ahistorical addition indicating Paul's importance in the formation of the church.

Looking again at the Pentecost account in Acts, there are two aspects of it that are not often emphasized, but deserve our mention. The first is Peter's promise to those who receive the message he proclaims: "you shall receive the gift of the Holy Spirit" (Acts 2:38). Keeping in mind what we have said above about the role of the Spirit in transforming those who seek to follow the way of Jesus, this assertion is not to be overlooked. Repentance (change of heart) and baptism for the forgiveness of sins are not ends in themselves, according to Acts. A life in the Spirit, which—as we have seen—means the gradual process of being "changed into [Christ's] image from glory to glory," is the primary goal for those converted.

The second aspect in Acts 2 to note is the Spirit's work of forming a sacramental, prayerful, learning community of equality and sharing: "And they devoted themselves to the apostles' teaching and fellowship, to the breaking of bread and the [communal] prayers . . . And all who believed were together and had all things in common; and they sold their possessions and goods and distributed them to all, as any had need" (Acts 2:42, 44–45). In other words, the coming of the Spirit is both for personal transformation and the formation of a true disciple-community.

We have had two millennia of failures and some successes in both these areas. The world still awaits a Christian community whose life is clearly lived "in the Spirit," where love and equality are the standard, where all races and types of people are welcome, where material goods are shared and no difference between rich and poor is tolerated, and where disciples are taught a truly transformative spiritual life. We have seen glimpses of it in the course of Christian history; but now that we are witnessing the demise of Constantinian Christendom, perhaps we may hope for a renewal of the original vision of Christ. Perhaps a "new Pentecost" will come our way and a more profound—perhaps less ordered, less regulated, more diverse, more Jesus-centered, more attuned to the Spirit—spirituality will energize a reawakened church.

The Nineteenth Mystery

The Assumption of Mary

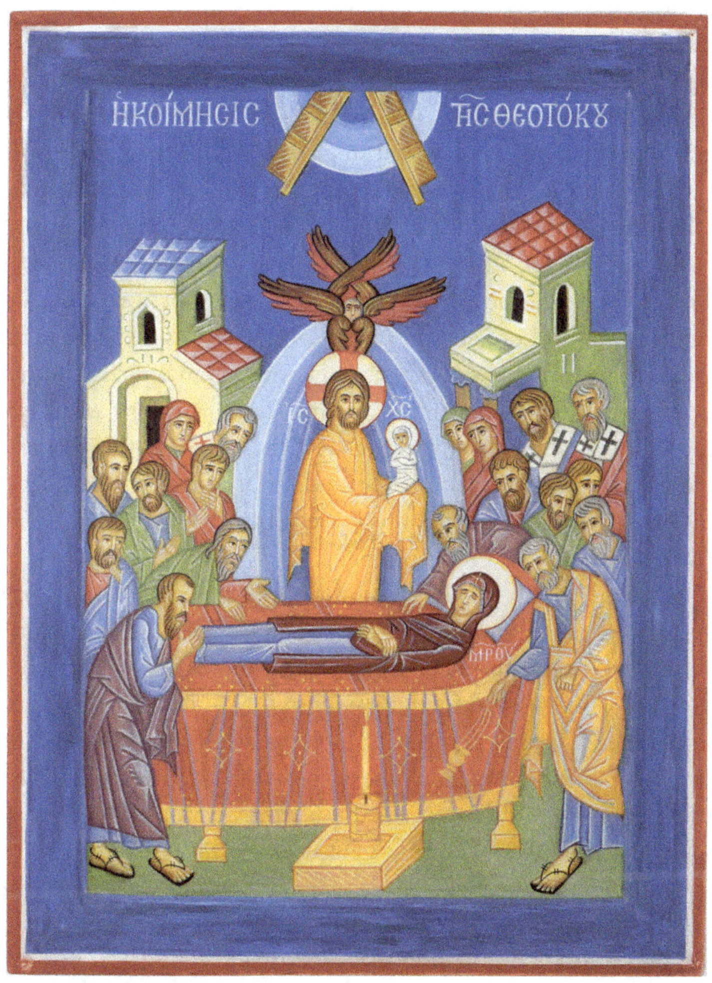

Readings for reflection:

> John 5:25; 11:25–26; 14:1-3; Romans 8:11; 1 Corinthians 15:42–57; Philippians 3:20–21

The final two mysteries of the rosary are not taken directly from Scripture but grew naturally out of early traditions concerning the meaning of Mary, the virgin mother of Christ. In a literal sense they have to do with the "historical" Mary; but, in their fuller spiritual sense, they have to do with the "virgin mother church," of which Mary is perhaps the foremost image.

As we have indicated before, what is reflected in miniature in the stories—both canonical and apocryphal—about the life of Mary is the universal life of the church. The "church"—in Greek, *ekklesia*—is God's "called-out assembly," the root and stock of which is the people of Israel, from whom Jesus was born. Grafted into this stock, to use Paul's analogy, were the other peoples of the earth through Christ, joining into one many races and nations (cf. Rom 11:17–24). Mary, in a sense, was the physical "bridge" between the Old and New Covenants, between the Israelite church awaiting her Lord and the universal church fulfilled in her Lord. In Mary the church is depicted symbolically, and in that typological capacity her death and what lay beyond it became significant for the developing tradition. The rosary, a late addition to Christian devotion historically, but growing out of this much older reading of Mary's significance, thus rounds out its series of meditations by returning to the source of Christ's incarnate humanity: his virgin mother.

The theme of "exchange" has always been fundamental to Christian belief. "He became what we are so that we might become what he is" is a phrase that has been expressed in one way or another down the centuries. The Word of God assumed full humanity so that humanity could "become divine by grace." On the cross, Christ took upon himself the sins of the human race so that humanity might be accorded the status of sinlessness. By his resurrection, the power of death was broken and human beings possess the hope of sharing God's own life. One aspect of this exchange is pictured in the traditional comparison of the iconography of the "virgin birth" of Jesus with that of the "Assumption" (the "taking up") of Mary. As Christ entered into the ebb and flow of time by "assuming" human nature from the virgin mother, so it was that when the time of her departure came, he took her "up" to share in his eternal glory. The Assumption of Mary, then, is a traditional image of victory over death through the agency of Christ. An older name for this mystery is the "Dormition" (the "falling asleep") of the Virgin. It was originally a commemoration of her death and burial, as well as her entrance into paradise. The mythological story of the event, fleshed out and embroidered in the fifth and sixth centuries, tells of her death and of the miraculous conveying of the apostles from the ends of the earth to her bier. Subsequently, according to one version, upon opening her tomb it was discovered that her body had also been assumed to heaven.[13]

The iconography of the Dormition is particularly touching, as we can note with our icon here. Still the common artistic representation in eastern Christianity today, it was once the universal motif of the Assumption, as common in the medieval West as it was in the Byzantine East. Without touching on all the icon's various details, at the center of it is pictured the apostles, including Paul, gathered about the reposing Virgin. Above this earthly scene we see Christ, bearing in his arms towards the open portals of heaven the tiny, infant-like figure of Mary. She is wrapped in white linen bands, intentionally reminiscent of the swaddling bands in which Mary had wrapped the infant Christ in the cave of the nativity (see the icon of the third mystery above). The motif both mirrors and inverts the image of Mary holding the infant Lord. Here it is she who is the "infant," newly born into eternal life. Her smallness and her bindings visually heighten the sense of her absolute dependence on Jesus for her Assumption. This feature of her helplessness to rise from death without Christ's power to free her from it was lost to Western art with the Renaissance. Later Western depictions of the Assumption have her superhumanly ascending into glory—"on her own steam," so to speak. This was a sad development, undermining the point of the mythological motif and, in fact, the essential Christological thread of the "salvation story." But there is nothing so troublingly goddess-like in the traditional icon. There, instead, she is tiny, dependent, creaturely: "I have calmed and quieted my soul, like a child quieted at its mother's breast; like a child that is quieted is my soul. O Israel, hope in the Lord from this time forth and for evermore" (Ps 131:2–3).

In this representation, therefore, we find an emphasis on the concept of grace. Grace is unmerited, a gift of God. Without it there could be no victory over death and sin and no ascent into the glory of God. Mary on her "own steam" could accomplish nothing more than any other human being where mortality was concerned. She had no power to save herself from the grave and no inherent prestige that had not been given to her by grace. She had to be "assumed" by the divine power of Christ. This icon, then, depicts visually what Christ had said to his hearers: "Truly, truly, I say to you, the hour is coming, and now is, when the dead will hear the voice of the Son of God, and those who hear will live . . . I am the resurrection and the life . . . Let not

13. One particularly worthwhile little book pertaining to this subject is Daley, *On the Dormition of Mary*.

your hearts be troubled; believe in God, believe also in me . . . When I go and prepare a place for you, I will come again and will take you to myself, that where I am you may be also" (John 5:25; 11:25; 14:1, 3).

The church, of which Mary is the image, also does nothing on its "own steam." Like Mary, the disciples of Jesus are dependent on grace: "Apart from me you can do nothing" (John 15:5). Mary, her trust (which is what "faith" means) vindicated and carried childlike in the arms of Christ, is a symbol of the church's and corporate humanity's utter dependence—and each human being's personal dependence, as well—on the gift of God. On the personal psychological level, until we reach the mature realization of our own fragility and mortality, our impermanence and that of the world's, and that our lives are a continuum from infant helplessness through struggles and defeats to (should we live so long) the helplessness of old age and finally death, we will have no appreciation of the reality of our own dependence and need for grace. The Dormition, it should be evident, is a picture of trust in the face of the unknown. Spiritually, as well, we wait in silence, dependent on the Spirit to awaken within us a perception of reality. It is an "assumption" out of "sleep" that we undergo in those moments when God's presence is inwardly encountered in our practice. At such moments, we recommit our lives—and approaching deaths—to God's care.

All this constitutes dependence on God's grace in the face of unpredictability, instability, fragility, sorrow, and death. It is beautifully pictured for us in the icon of an infant Mary, absolutely trusting and dependent, held in the arms of Christ and assumed by him to share in his glory.

The Twentieth Mystery

The Coronation of Mary

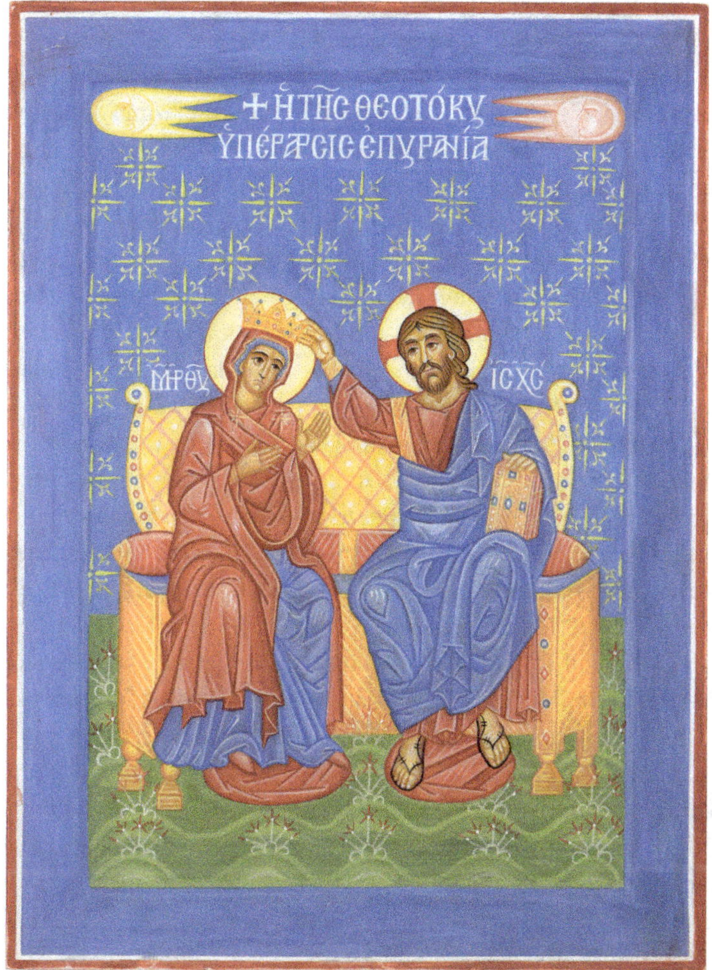

Readings for reflection:

> Luke 1:43; Revelation 12:1–6; 21:2, 9–10; John 17:1–5, 22; Romans 8: 15–17, 28–30; 1 Corinthians 15:22–28; 2 Corinthians 3:18; Ephesians 2:5–6; 2 Peter 1:4; 1 John 3:1–3

The image of Mary enthroned in the glory of her Son, which is the final mystery of the rosary, brings the series full circle. Like the depiction of the Dormition/Assumption, in which an "infant" Mary carried in the arms of Christ inverts the nativity imagery of the infant Christ in the arms of his mother, the "Coronation" image inverts the imagery of the Annunciation, the first of the mysteries. The Annunciation icon, as you will recall, shows us the Word, descended into and enclosed within the womb of his mother. The Coronation icon reverses this; in it, Mary has been taken up into and is encompassed by the glory of her divine Son. She is shown to be "deified" or "divinized" by grace, to use the language of the ancient Eastern theologians and mystics. In her role as the premier symbol of the church, she is presented here as foreshadowing the ultimate destiny of redeemed humanity, as this was understood within the classical tradition of Christianity.

As we saw in the second mystery, the Visitation of Mary to Elizabeth, Mary was hailed in "queenly" fashion in Elizabeth's exclamation (Luke 1:43). The phrase "Mother of the Lord" had a meaning that was unmistakable within its cultural context. A nation's queen was understood to be the king's mother, not his bride (cf. Luke 1:30–33; also, see the example of the high regard accorded to Bathsheba by her own son, King Solomon, in 1 Kgs 2:19–20). This same motif underlies the mysterious figure of the Woman in Revelation 12. This resplendent figure, evidently the symbol for both Israel and the church embodied in a single image, is described as a glorified Mother who gives birth to the Messiah and is crowned as "Queen Mother" with twelve stars (possibly the twelve constellations). The Woman is a sign of the church as both glorious and also persecuted. Implicitly, there is a shared identity between this "Woman clothed with the sun" and the glorious New Jerusalem, "the Bride of the Lamb," in the final chapters of the book of Revelation. In this matrix of apocalyptic symbolism, the church (redeemed humanity) is at once virgin, mother, and bride.

It is a small step conceptually from this New Testament background to the traditional image of Mary crowned and glorified, the personification of final union between God and redeemed humanity. She is also the image of each member of the body, raised up and glorified—deified—by God's grace. In the church's tradition, the image of the glorified Mary is the representation of humanity's intended destiny: "It does not yet appear what we shall be, but we know that when he appears we shall be like him, for we shall see him as he is" (1 John 3:2). The mystery of Mary's "Coronation," then, points beyond Mary as an individual person to all humanity's completion or true end. The image is unabashedly teleological in nature—*telos* meaning that there is a "goal" or "end" toward which creation is being drawn. That goal is called by Paul "glory"—and it is the destiny of all to be "changed into the same image [of Christ] from glory to glory, even as by the Spirit of the Lord" (2 Cor 3:18 KJV).

This, of course, forces the question of whether or not we truly can aspire to a transcendent goal as the destiny of human existence. Is such a hope credible? Christians certainly dare to say that it is, as do the other great faiths of humankind in their various ways. Such a hopeful conviction is often countered with the hardheaded objection, posed by some scientists and philosophical materialists, that we are all really just "naked apes," a particularly intelligent primate species that has achieved comparatively much in a random, meaningless universe, and happily situated at the top of the food chain for the time being—"monkeys with money and guns," in Tom Waits's memorable phrase. Admittedly, to refer to human beings as "naked apes" comes across as insulting to human dignity, but it is—to give the devil his due—another way of saying something that Christians have forthrightly acknowledged from the beginning. To admit that human beings are small, insignificant, often absurd, more animal than angel, psychologically fragile and floundering, and so on, is nothing new. Jesus said as much when he diagnosed the human "heart" (Mark 7:17–23). And yet, there really is no reason at all to accept meekly that our existence has no final meaning or destiny. Such a dispiriting assumption is no more an empirically verifiable conclusion than its opposite. To affirm one or the other is a matter of faith—"science" has nothing to say on the matter and "hardheaded realism" can be as stubbornly delusional as religious hysteria.

Regarding, then, the Christian hope for humanity, the philosopher and theologian John Hick summed it up in this way: "The *telos* to which our existence is directed can be formally described as human perfection, man's full humanization, the total realization of the potentialities of finite personal life or, in the daring language of eastern orthodox Christianity, man's divinization."[14] The Christian view is that creation in its present state is unfinished and unfulfilled. We might say it is only half-baked, not yet having reached the end for which it was made. Paul wrote that that end would be reached when God is finally "all in all" (1 Cor 15:28)—a *telos*, it must be said, that cannot be adequately expressed or even imagined this side of things. "For the creation was subjected to futility," he says encouragingly elsewhere,

14. Hick, *Death and Eternal Life*, 407.

"not of its own will but by the will of [God] who subjected it in hope; because the creation itself will be set free from its bondage to decay and obtain the glorious liberty of the children of God" (Rom 8:20–21).

Human destiny and human frailty are both intimately related to the conditions of material nature; and, if we dare to say it in these terms, from our position in "spacetime," the formless chaotic elements of Genesis 1 have not yet been completely transformed by God's "glory." That is to say, "nature" as we experience it in the flow of time is still a work in progress. It has not yet been fully shaped and finished. The "first fruits" of the completed work is what we see accomplished in Christ, resurrected and glorified. Paul renders this otherwise inexpressible vision in the mythological language of apocalypse:

> For as in Adam all die, so also in Christ shall all be made alive. But each in his own order: Christ the first fruits, then at his coming those who belong to Christ. Then comes the end, when he delivers the kingdom to God the Father after destroying every rule and every authority and power. For he must reign until he has put all his enemies under his feet. The last enemy to be destroyed is death . . . When all things are subjected to him, then the Son himself will also be subjected to him [the Father] who put all things under him, that God may be all in all. (1 Cor 15:22–26, 28)

The "glory" of God in Scripture, when that word (*doxa*) is not referring to "praise" or "honor," is the radiance of God himself, the uncreated light. It is God's own presence and power, an expression of his *physis* or "nature." It would appear that Paul and also the Johannine writings mean by our sharing in "the glory of God" what 2 Peter 1:4 means when it says that, in Christ, believers have "become partakers of the divine *nature*." The classical Christian term for this transformative union with God's "glory" and "nature" is *theosis*—which we have translated above as "deification" and "divinization"; and it means that human destiny is "to become by grace what Christ [or God] is by nature." Or, as that irascible but brilliant Greek father, Athanasius of Alexandria (c. 297–373), put it, "He was humanized so that we might be deified";[15] or, again, in the daring words of Basil of Caesarea (330–379), the Holy Spirit lifts up the believer—and note the three levels of the gradual ascent "from glory to glory" he demarcates—to "abide in God, to be made like God, and, highest of all, to become God."[16] In Paul's

15. Athanasius, *On the Incarnation of the Word*, ch. 54, 3.

16. Basil, *On the Holy Spirit*, ch. 9, 23.

language, this participation in God's glory means to be "heirs of God and fellow heirs with Christ" (Rom 8: 17); in John's language, "the glory given" to us is the same glory which the Son shared with the Father "before the world was made" (John 17:22, 25). To participate in "the glory of God" means, ultimately, we will be enabled wholly and freely to cooperate in the dignity, knowledge, and action of the Godhead. It goes without saying that such an exalted future condition is beyond all human ability to envision in the present: "Eye has not seen, nor ear heard, nor the heart of man conceived, what God has prepared for those who love him" (1 Cor 2:9). We might even render this in terms of human "consciousness" being raised up gradually until coming to realize its oneness with the "universal consciousness" of God that underlies and fills all reality—a realization we can merely glimpse from time to time in our work of silence.

In this understanding of things, the comparative smallness of our planet in the Milky Way, which is just one galaxy among hundreds of billions, the shortness and seeming unimportance of our earthly lives, the billions of years between the beginning of the universe and the first appearance of the human species (as well as the relative brevity of our species' existence on this planet when compared to the many millions of years of previous animal existence), the quantum randomness that exists in the order of the things we perceive, and so on—in other words, all those things which seem to argue so persuasively for the irrelevance of the human race—in reality have no bearing whatsoever on the actuality that is yet to be. If humankind is destined to become "like God," whatever that reality will entail or look like, then we will evolve "from glory to glory" to comprehend the entire universe from God's own eternal perspective. We will not question the microscopic origins of our existence from a tiny and temporal world any more than we now question our origins from sperm and egg. To be "like God"—to "be made God" by grace—would be an exaltation of our consciousness beyond all human thought in our present condition to comprehend.

But the reality that exceeds our imagination can still be given significant form in mythology and art. The image of Mary enthroned, crowned, and exalted is one such image. The Virgin Mother glorified was, in both the Christian East and Christian West, the vision of humanity perfected and "clothed" in splendor. And, in our cycle of mysteries, if the mystery of the Annunciation was the "womb" from which all the subsequent mysteries come, the mystery of the Coronation is their consummation. In our icon, which in this case is a Western motif rendered in an Eastern style, we have Christ and the Virgin Mother, seated among the stars, sun, and moon above them in attendance, sharing a common throne. The viewer needs to understand, of course, that this is not an instance of "Mariolatry." She is not to be understood in a literalist way as the subject of the picture. She is a symbol, a representation both of the church (or collective humanity) and each human person elevated in Christ. Mary visually signifies here the spiritual status that scripture says pertains to all who are in Christ: God "made us alive together with Christ (by grace you have been saved), and raised us up with him, and *made us sit with him in the heavenly places* in Christ Jesus" (Eph 2:5–6; emphasis added); "I will come again and will take you to myself, that where I am you may be also" (John 14:3). Mary symbolizes in the icon those who have "become partakers of the divine nature" (2 Pet 1:4), fulfilling the promise made in the First Letter of John that "we shall be like him, for we shall see him as he is" (1 John 3:2). Once again, the goal of the incarnation (God humanized) is God's glory (humanity deified). The image of the naked ape has been supplanted by that of the coronated Mary, the figure of deified humanity. We could also say, as regards the practice of contemplation, that it also mythologically depicts our consciousness lifted up and united with God's.

It is, in summary, in that enigmatic figure of "the Woman clothed with the sun" that we have an icon of the beginning and end of our salvation. In this traditional image of Mary's glorification in Christ, we have a sign of human destiny's perfect form. It is the Christian vision, the reality of which exceeds all pictorial art or human imagining. In this mystery we are given a reminder that "our knowledge is imperfect and our prophecy is imperfect; but when the perfect comes, the imperfect will pass away . . . [and] then I shall understand fully, even as I have been fully understood" (1 Cor 13:9–10, 12). If God can so love the naked ape, that all-too-frequently unlovely species, and reshape its raw and disagreeable stuff into the beauty we see epitomized in the archetypal and eschatological Woman clothed with the sun, Mary the "queen of heaven," then we might reserve hope for ourselves and also for each and every human being.

Salve Regina, Mater misericordiae; vita dulcedo et spes nostra salve.

Bibliography

Adam of Perseigne. "Sermon 5, On the Assumption." Translated by Philip O'Mara. *Cistercian Studies Quarterly* 33.2 (1998) 151–63.

Athanasius. *On the Incarnation of the Word*. In vol. 4 of *Nicene and Post-Nicene Fathers* (Second Series), edited by Philip Schaff and Henry Wallace. Peabody, MA: Hendrickson, 1999.

Barker, Margaret. *Christmas: The Original Story*. London: SPCK, 2008.

———. *Temple Mysticism: An Introduction*. London: SPCK, 2011.

Basil the Great. *On the Spirit*. In vol. 8 of *Nicene and Post-Nicene Fathers* (Second Series), edited by Philip Schaff and Henry Wallace. Peabody, MA: Hendrickson, 1999.

Blakney, Raymond Bernard. *Meister Eckhart: A Modern Translation*. New York: Harper and Brothers, 1941.

The Book of Common Prayer: 1662 Version (includes the 1549 Version and other commemorations). Introduction by Diarmaid MacCulloch. London: Everyman's Library, 1999.

Cartlidge, D. R., and J. K. Elliott. *Art and the Christian Apocrypha*. London: Routledge, 2001.

Charlesworth, James H., ed. *The Old Testament Pseudepigrapha, Volume 1*. Garden City, NY: Doubleday, 1983.

———. *The Old Testament Pseudepigrapha, Volume 2*. Garden City, NY: Doubleday, 1985.

Crossan, John Dominic, and Sarah Sexton Crossan. *Resurrecting Easter: How the West Lost and the East Kept the Original Easter Vision*. New York: HarperCollins, 2018.

Daley, Brian E., SJ, ed. *On the Dormition of Mary: Early Patristic Homilies*. Crestwood, NY: St. Vladimir's Seminary Press, 1998.

The Gospel of Nicodemus, Greek form. In vol. 8 of *Ante-Nicene Fathers*. Peabody, MA: Hendrickson, 1999.

Harris, Peter, ed. *Zen Poems*. New York: Knopf, 1999.

Hart, Addison Hodges. *The Ox-Herder and the Good Shepherd: Finding Christ on the Buddha's Path*. Grand Rapids: Eerdmans, 2013.

———. *The Woman, the Hour, and the Garden: A Study of Imagery in the Gospel of John*. Grand Rapids: Eerdmans, 2016.

Hart, David Bentley. *The New Testament: A Translation*. New Haven, CT: Yale University Press, 2017.

Hennecke, Edgar, ed. *New Testament Apocrypha (Volume One: Gospels and Related Writings)*. Edited by Wilhelm Schneemelcher (English translation edited by R. McL. Wilson). Philadelphia: Westminster, 1963.

Hick, John. *Death and Eternal Life*. Glasgow: Collins Sons & Co., 1979.

Huizinga, Johan. *The Autumn of the Middle Ages*. Translated by Rodney J. Payton and Ulrich Mammitzsch. Chicago: University of Chicago Press, 1996.

Ignatius of Antioch. *Letter to the Ephesians*. In *Apostolic Fathers I*, edited and translated by Kirsopp Lake, 192–93. Cambridge, MA: Harvard University Press, 1935.

Irenaios. *The Preaching of the Apostles*. Prepared by Jack N. Sparks. Brookline, MA: Holy Cross Orthodox, n. d.

John-Julian, Fr., OJN. *The Complete Julian of Norwich*. Brewster, MA: Paraclete, 2009.

Levine Amy-Jill, and Marc Zvi Brettler, eds. *The Jewish Annotated New Testament*. New York: Oxford University Press, 2011.

The Liturgy of the Hours According to the Roman Rite. Volume II (Lenten Season/Easter Season). New York: Catholic Book Publishing, 1976.

MacCulloch, Diarmaid. *Christianity: The First Three Thousand Years*. New York: Penguin, 2009.

Meyer, Marvin, ed. *The Nag Hammadi Scriptures*. The International Edition. New York: HarperCollins, 2007.

Nes, Solrunn. *The Mystical Language of Icons*. Grand Rapids: Eerdmans, 1993.

———. *The Uncreated Light: An Iconographical Study of the Transfiguration in the Eastern Church*. Grand Rapids: Eerdmans, 2007.

Olivelle, Patrick, trans. *Upanishads*. New York: Oxford University Press, 1996.

Origen. *Commentary on the Gospel of John*. In vol. 9. of *Ante-Nicene Fathers*. Peabody, MA: Hendrickson, 1999.

———. *The Song of Songs: Commentary and Homilies*. Ancient Christian Writers 26. Translated and annotated by R. P. Lawson. Mahwah, NJ: Newman, 1956.

Pageau, Jonathan. "The Cave in the Nativity Icon." *Orthodox Arts Journal* (December 21, 2013). https://www.orthodoxartsjournal.org/the-cave-in-the-nativity-icon/.

Rahner, Hugo, SJ. *Our Lady and the Church*. Translated by Sebastian Bullough, OP. Chicago: Regnery, 1965.

Ross, Maggie. *Silence: A User's Guide (Volume 1: Process)*. Eugene, OR: Cascade, 2014.

———. *Silence: A User's Guide (Volume 2: Application)*. Eugene, OR: Cascade, 2018.

Tauler, Johannes. *The Inner Way: Being Thirty-Six Sermons for Festivals by John Tauler, Friar-Preacher of Strasburg*. A new translation from the German, edited with an Introduction by Arthur Wollaston Hutton, M.A., Rector of Easthope, Salop. London: Methuen & Co., n.d.

Toal, M. F., ed. and trans. *The Sunday Sermons of the Great Fathers: 1. From the First Sunday of Advent to Quinquagesima*. London: Longmans, Green, 1957.

Wright, J. Robert. *Readings for the Daily Office from the Early Church*. New York: Church Publishing, 1991.

www.ingramcontent.com/pod-product-compliance
Lightning Source LLC
LaVergne TN
LVHW050536100826
845148LV00002B/583

* 9 7 8 1 7 2 5 2 7 2 3 2 3 *